T0273664

THE MILLION DOLLAR MAN

THE MILLION DOLLAR MAN
Jack Dempsey

by Thomas Brennan

REGENT PRESS
Berkeley, California

Paperback
ISBN 13: 978-1-58790-401-1
ISBN 10: 1-58790-401-2

E-book:
ISBN 13: 978-1-58790-402-8
ISBN 10: 1-58790-402-0

Library of Congress Control Number: 2017939255

First Edition

0 1 2 3 4 5 6 7 8 9 10

Photo Credits:
Cover, pages 22 & 23 / *public domain*
Page 8 / *gettyimages*
All other photos / *Alamy Stock Photos*

Manufactured in the United States of America

REGENT PRESS
www.regentpress.net
regentpress@mindspring.com

CONTENTS

INTRODUCTION

JACK DEMPSEY. The very name conjures up a sense of ferociousness, savagery, excitement, and above all, deep-seated respect. The very thoughts that must have passed through the minds of many an adversary who dared face Jack in the ring.

Dempsey may not have defended his title as frequently as Joe Louis, and he may not have been as defensively skilled and agile as Muhammad Ali. But he was by far the most exciting and colorful heavyweight champion ever to have strapped on a pair of boxing gloves. Dempsey epitomized the very essence of the Roaring Twenties like no other figure in that turbulent and overindulgent decade.

Jack Dempsey is America's first mega sports hero. His style of boxing had never been seen before in the annals of pugilism. Dempsey ushered in the modern era of boxing. He singlehandedly brought shock and awe to the sport of boxing like no one before or since.

The Manassa Mauler backed down to no man in the ring. He stalked his opponents much the same way a tiger stalks his prey. Great champions had their own distinct style of boxing. Joe Louis waited patiently for an opening before landing blows with deadly accuracy. Muhammad Ali danced around his adversaries as he pummeled them with lightning fast jabs and right-crosses. And as he grew older he frequently utilized "rope-a-dope" as a way of tiring out his opponent. Not so with Dempsey. Jack created his own openings by swarming all over his adversary, thus causing his opponent to make regretful and costly mistakes.

Dempsey was instrumental in creating the first million-dollar gate. And not just one, but five of them. No other sports figure caused as much excitement and hysteria as Jack Dempsey did in the 1920s. Babe Ruth was so inspired by Dempsey's popularity, he seriously considered becoming a boxer.

In 1950 a highly respected and distinguished group of sportswriters and sportscasters voted Jack Dempsey as the greatest prizefighter in the first half of the twentieth century. In 1954 he was elected to the Boxing Hall of Fame.

Jack Dempsey left home when he was only fifteen in search of a new beginning. He found it in the rough and tumble mining towns scattered throughout Utah and Colorado. In between grueling jobs as a miner, Dempsey fought anyone and everyone. He won most of his fights but unfortunately his boxing career eventually stalled.

Then in 1917, Jack Dempsey's and Jack "Doc" Kearns' paths crossed either by fate or by accident. Under Kearns' tutelage, Dempsey's career took off so quickly that by early 1919, Dempsey had clearly become the top heavyweight contender. That same year, Dempsey annihilated champion Jess Willard in three rounds to become the new heavyweight king. The savage beating Jess Willard suffered in the first three minutes of the fight is considered by many to be the worst punishment ever received in a single round by a heavyweight champion.

In 1921, Dempsey defended his title for the third time. And the first million-dollar gate was born. The "Fight of the Century" pitted Jack against a very successful and popular French war hero named Georges Carpentier. The spectacle drew dozens of dignitaries and celebrities from around the world. The challenger gave it his all, but in the end, he succumbed to Dempsey's dreaded assault in the fourth round.

In 1923, Dempsey defended his title against the very dangerous and lethal fighter, Luis Angel Firpo. The Argentinian was crude but he was huge and immensely powerful and he was very adept at hammering his opponents into submission. The Dempsey-Firpo fight would go down in history as the second million-dollar gate. The fight appeared over when Firpo knocked Dempsey out of the ring in the first round. Dempsey came storming back and knocked out the "Wild Bull of the Pampas" in the very next round. The fight is considered by many to be the most exciting heavyweight championship contest in history.

Dempsey returned to defend his title after a three-year absence from the ring. In 1926, Jack faced an up and coming, brilliant boxer by the name of Gene Tunney. The event would become the third million-dollar gate. Dempsey's long layoff proved to be his undoing. He lost a ten-round decision to Tunney in a stunning upset.

In 1927, Dempsey battled Jack Sharkey in the first non-title fight to rake in over a million dollars, making it the fourth million-dollar gate. Behind in points, Dempsey knocked out Sharkey in the seventh round in a highly controversial fight. That same year, Dempsey faced Tunney again in yet another million-dollar gate bout. Dempsey lost the decision to Tunney, prompting the Manassa Mauler to wisely announce his retirement from the ring.

Jack Dempsey left behind a remarkable fight record. He reportedly knocked out 26 adversaries in the first round, a feat perhaps unequaled in the heavyweight division. He achieved a very high knockout rate of 59 percent. In 2003, *Ring* magazine rated him the seventh greatest puncher of all time. But more importantly than Jack's fight record, he remains one of the most admired and beloved sports figures of any era.

CHAPTER ONE

ON THE MOVE

Jack poses with his parents Celia and Hyrum Dempsey.

Jack Dempsey's father, Hyrum Dempsey, was a descendant of hard working Irish immigrants from County Kildare, Ireland. Many of them came to America in the 1700s. Some of Hyrum's ancestors settled in Logan County, West Virginia. The county was commonly referred to as "feud country" due to the notorious war between the Hatfields and the McCoys. In fact, Hyrum had the dubious distinction of being a nephew of "Devil" Anse Hatfield. Anse Hatfield proudly passed on his motto, "Never kick a cripple or go to bed with a fool" to Hyrum.

Jack's paternal grandfather, Andrew Dempsey, was Logan County's sheriff. He was also the county surveyor. He was respectfully known as "Big Andy" or "Big Dempsey." Hyrum was the oldest of Andrew's five offspring, all of whom were male. "Big Andy" was bitterly disappointed by the fact that all of his sons were significantly physically smaller in stature than he was.

The population of rugged Logan County consisted primarily of Irish and Anglo-Saxon stock. While residing in Logan County, Hyrum met and fell in love with a young, independent minded girl named Mary Celia Smoot. She was Scotch-Irish and hailed from West Virginia. Celia was also part Cherokee Indian. Jack remembered his mother was able "to see and hear things the rest of us couldn't." Celia was a cousin of Reed Smoot, a U.S. senator from Utah.

Celia was a tomboy who loved to ride horses bareback. Hyrum was immediately attracted to her sense of independence and physical beauty. Celia was not particularly interested in what Hyrum had to offer, however. She was interested in someone who was as spirited and independent minded as she was.

Jack claimed the Dempsey clan had a "strain of Choctaw Indian blood." Moreover, the Dempseys were reportedly related to the Vances, another notorious mountaineer family known for their deadly feuds in Kentucky and West Virginia.

Celia's father owned and operated a dry goods store in Logan County. According to Jack, his mother's father convinced her that Hyrum was a good man. After several years of courtship, Hyrum and Celia finally married sometime in 1868 in Logan County. The two struggled because they had very little money. Hyrum suffered from an unrelenting urge to quickly strike it rich. He was not able to hold down a job for very long. Because of this, the young couple quarreled constantly.

Hyrum drank very heavily at times. He never had much money but when he did have some, he'd imbibe. When he wasn't busy drinking himself into a stupor, he would sit back in his favorite chair and play the fiddle. He particularly enjoyed playing "Turkey in the Straw."

Hyrum managed to get a position as a teacher at a local schoolhouse in Mud Fork, West Virginia. His one year of college probably helped him obtain such a responsible position. He detested his job, however. Jack remembered his father declaring, "All a teacher needs to know is something you don't. If one is smart enough, he'll learn to ask lots of questions and notice things around him. Observation — that's all it is — observation."

Hyrum had grown thoroughly disgusted with his job after four years of teaching. He even seriously considered terminating his livelihood. One day he heard that a traveling missionary preacher would soon be arriving in town. The preacher was a Mormon and he was coming all the way from Salt Lake City, Utah.

The preacher excitedly informed the locals that "there's a new life out west, a new opportunity to start fresh…" Hyrum desperately wanted to head out to the promised land. Celia wanted to move there as well, but for an entirely different reason. She liked what she heard about the Mormon teachings. Hyrum and Celia converted to this new religion and the family headed west. Dempsey recalled his father's "face was turned toward the west, I think, all his life."

Jack's mother was deeply religious and did her best to instill that same passion in her children. She read stories from the Bible and made sure all of her children said their prayers. Jack recalled he was taught that a "worthy life is measured by knowing the difference between right and wrong." Hyrum, on the other hand, didn't embrace the Bible as fervently as his wife. Dempsey later learned his father was much more interested in what he could get out of the here and now, not from the hereafter.

Hyrum, who had just turned twenty-five, decided to sell all the real estate he had inherited. At first, he had difficulty selling his land. Finally, he was offered one dollar an acre for 300 acres. He thought the offer was much too low, but he accepted it anyhow. Hyrum sold some timberland he had inherited from his grandfather and bought horses and a large covered wagon. Hyrum loaded up the wagon with provisions and his family and headed west.

The family suffered tremendous hardship along the way. Frequently, the children were told to hang on together on one side of the wagon in order to keep it from tipping over. In other instances, their water ran out and they were forced to dig wells in order to survive. They passed many dead animals along the way which suggested just how dangerous their journey actually was. The Dempseys persevered nonetheless.

The family settled in a little town called Manassa, Colorado. Hyrum accepted a low paying job cutting and hauling timber. Hyrum's boss, Hugh Sellers, was amazed at the amount of food Hyrum could consume in one sitting. "Hyrum Dempsey," Sellers liked to relate, "could eat more than any man alive. Never saw such an eater for a man his size. And he wasn't afraid of anything in the world. Once I had to keep him from fighting a big she-bear with an ax."

William Harrison Dempsey was born on June 24, 1895, in Manassa, Colorado. He was named after President William Harrison. Apparently, naming newborns after presidents was popular in those days. The midwife who had assisted with the delivery was paid twenty-five cents. Jack was a big baby, tipping the scales at eleven pounds. He was the ninth child to be born to the Dempseys. Hyrum and Celia would eventually have thirteen children.

Many years later Jack reminisced about his early childhood in a book called *Dempsey*. "It had been a rugged childhood," he recalled. "An old story perhaps, but a painful one; too many mouths to feed, a father with the wanderlust and almost no ability to make a decent living, a mother who performed all a wife's chores and saw to all of her husband's responsibilities. It was the kind of life that had sent me on the road as soon as I could get away. As it had sent my older brothers and sisters."

Jack's mother cared deeply for her children. According to Jack, Celia was a realist, unlike his father. She was strict and nobody's fool. One time, however, she allowed a gypsy to foretell her future. The gypsy insisted Celia lend her a silver dollar. She placed the coin under her tongue "to help the spell." When the gypsy claimed that the dollar had mysteriously vanished, Celia threatened to do bodily harm to her. The gypsy promptly returned the dollar and quickly moved on to her next victim.

Before Jack was born, his mother had read a book given to her by an old peddler. The name of the book was *Life of a 19th Century Gladiator*. The author was the great John L. Sullivan, America's first heavyweight champion. She read the book over and over again. She told Jack many years later that, before he was born, she wanted her next male child to be the next John L. Sullivan.

Jack remembered quite clearly his childhood in Manassa. He recalled that "my mother was too crowded with work, and my father too busy with his own schemes and expeditions, to have much time for us. We had to be shaped by our day-to-day-adventures and experiences, the fights with Mexican boys, and trying to throw ropes on horses, rather than by much guidance from our parents. There was little discipline of any kind. But although my mother never babied us, we could always sense her boundless affection for us. Someway, it meant a lot. We never had any 'store toys.' We had to make our own playthings. Chips of wood became boats, sticks became spears, bits of old rope became lariats. We were able to make fairly respectable bows and arrows. We had a lot of fun with these things."

When Jack was seven he fought with a neighbor boy

named Fred Daniels. The two boys swung at each other, trying desperately to knock the other down. Adults stood around the boys hollering and laughing much to their amusement. The spectators were evidently starved for any kind of entertainment. Fred Daniels' father yelled at his son to bite Jack. Just as Fred turned to his father to hear what he had said, Jack landed a hard punch on Fred's chin. The boy fell to the ground, thus ending the brawl. Jack believed this incident had an important effect on his overall fighting strategy. As soon as you see an opening, take full advantage of it because another one may not come along. Whether Jack knew it or not, he was already preparing himself as a formidable fighter to be reckoned with.

Not too long after the Dempseys had settled in Manassa, Hyrum was fired from his farming job. Disillusioned, he decided it was time for the family to move on. The Dempseys headed to much higher elevations. Celia soon suffered from excruciating stomach pains and fainted several times during the long, treacherous climb up the mountains.

In June of 1904, the Dempseys moved to Uncompahgre, Colorado. According to Jack, the Indian name Uncompahgre meant "very beautiful." Hyrum hired himself out as a rancher's hand. It was a rough life for Jack and his siblings. Before going off to school, Jack and the rest of his family had to milk the cows, chop wood, collect eggs, and clear away horse manure.

The Dempseys had just settled into their new home when Hyrum lost his job. Once again Hyrum moved his family to their next surroundings, Montrose, Colorado. By this time Celia had had her fill of Hyrum's inability to hold down a job for very long. In order to make ends meet she ran a little restaurant called the Rio Grande Eating House. Initially, business was good for Celia because the railroad station was close by. Laborers traveled to Montrose to help construct the Gunnison Tunnel. The railroad hired hundreds of men to prepare the land so that rails and railroad ties could be installed.

Jack's mother always made sure her children learned practical lessons in morality. Celia taught her children the virtue of self-reliance and hard work. Hanging on the wall of their home was a plaque which read, "MAKE YOURSELF AN HONEST MAN — AND THEN YOU MAY BE SURE THERE IS ONE RASCAL LESS IN THE WORLD."

Jack landed a job in a barbershop where he shined customer's shoes and tidied up the place. Although he never read much, he liked to read the *Police Gazette*. There were many stories in the popular men's magazine about prize fighters. Jack imagined becoming a famous fighter one day, perhaps even the world heavyweight champion.

Jack had become an effective coyote trapper by the time he was twelve. He learned that trapping coyotes required patience and a lot of experience. Jack learned how to determine the coyote's favorite trails so he could lay traps. He discovered that smearing bait with animal blood helped hide human scent. Many of the techniques Jack utilized in capturing these animals were self-taught. At a very early age he had learned the importance of self-reliance. He later applied this essential trait when he began to seriously train as a fighter.

The entire family worked very hard clearing the land and making something out of their small farm. They worked from 6:00 am until dark. Jack learned to operate the mowing machine and helped rake and stack hay. He actually enjoyed working hard. He believed hard work helped him develop strong muscles and stamina. He dreamed of one day becoming a boxer like his older brother, Bernie.

The family consumed huge portions of food in order to increase and maintain their strength. Celia cooked enormous batches of chicken, Mexican beans, corn, bread, and potatoes. The family raised their own animal stock for slaughter. The Dempseys ate mainly pork, mutton, and veal. They ate wild honey because sugar was hard to come by.

Wild burros roamed the hills near the Dempsey household. Jack helped round-up the burros and lead them into a corral where they were broken. Some of the burros were used for riding and others were harnessed and sold. Jack learned to become an expert at roping and riding the wild burros.

Jack's older brother, Bernie, had become a boxer. Jack confided in Bernie that he too wanted to become a prize fighter. Bernie began teaching his younger brother the rudiments of boxing. Unfortunately, Bernie suffered from a glass chin. The handicap of not being able to take a hard punch to the jaw prevented Bernie from ever rising within the pugilistic ranks. Nevertheless, he was able to teach Jack quite a few tricks of the trade.

Bernie and Jack built a makeshift gymnasium from an old chicken coop. A punching bag was made from a cloth bag stuffed with sawdust. Jack was concerned about how skinny he looked. It worried him that he might not be able to get fights because of his small stature. Jack jumped rope in order to strengthen his leg muscles. By performing this important exercise, he hoped it would also improve his endurance in the ring.

Jack participated in a lot of sports activities in school. He excelled in baseball and basketball. He particularly liked basketball because it allowed him to improve his speed and agility. He became outstanding at track and field and he was considered one of the best sprinters and high jumpers in his school. Jack recalled that he ran the 100-yard dash in ten seconds, a remarkable feat.

Jack's interest in boxing really took hold around the time of the Jack Johnson vs Jim Jeffries world heavyweight bout in 1910. He drew an illustration of Jack Johnson on one side of his punching bag and an illustration of Jim Jeffries on the opposite side. He took turns pounding each side of the punching bag with incredible determination. After Johnson beat Jeffries, Jack drew a picture of Johnson over his drawing of Jeffries and pounded both sides of the bag unmercifully.

Very aware that a glass jaw was a sure ticket to oblivion in the fight world, Bernie always reminded Jack to chew pine gum in order to strengthen his jaw. Dempsey reluctantly chewed the harsh tasting pine gum because he detested the awful taste. Jack also soaked his face in beef brine in order to toughen his skin. Bernie claimed that the tougher the facial skin, the less chance a fighter could bleed from a cut. Bernie explained to his younger brother that a deep cut could unexpectedly end a fight.

Jack's family always referred to him as "Harry." That would all change after Jack substituted for his brother in a boxing match. Bernie went by the name of "Jack" whenever he participated in a bout, so Jack felt obligated to go by the name of "Jack" for the rest of his life.

Dempsey was very self-conscious about how poor his

family was. Although Jack always had plenty to eat, he still felt out of place with his schoolmates who were much better dressed than he was. Jack was determined not to be ridiculed for being poor for the rest of his life. He knew he needed to strike out on his own in order to gain respect.

With the completion of the Gunnison Tunnel, business suddenly slacked off at the Eatery. Hyrum and Celia sold their restaurant and moved to Provo, Utah where their family lived for a short time. The town was situated about forty miles due south of Salt Lake City. The Dempseys settled in Lakeview where Hyrum rented 120 acres of farm land.

Jack learned to hunt duck and quail. He trapped muskrats and sold their skins for as much as fifty-five cents per skin. He trapped rats that lived in the marshes and sold their skins as well. Jack also worked at a beet-sugar factory where he unloaded beets. He kept busy shoveling and plowing out furrows as well as weeding and hoeing the land.

Dempsey developed a fierce and unshakeable determination to become a championship prize fighter. He became even more resolved in his pursuit whenever anyone criticized his ambitious goal. One day Jack's eighth grade teacher, Ray Wentz, ridiculed Jack in front of his classmates. According to Jack, his teacher told him he would never amount to anything in life. The teacher warned him that he would be lucky to end up as a "dumb, uneducated wood-chopper." Shortly after his scolding Jack ran home and attacked his punching bag with a vengeance.

After Jack graduated from eighth grade, he decided he had had enough of schooling. At one point, however, he entertained the idea of attending high school and later Brigham Young University. He thought perhaps he would like to become a doctor. After all, he had helped his father successfully treat animals on his father's farm. But his aspirations of becoming a famous prize fighter dispelled any such notion. Jack explained to his parents that he was done with formal education and wanted to make a name for himself.

Jack traveled to Montrose to see some of his old friends. He boxed with them in order to determine if his fighting skills had improved. He returned home for short periods of time in order to help his father. He never stayed very long on the farm, however. One day Jack left the farm for good to begin his journey into the harsh, cruel world of life…and pugilism.

CHAPTER TWO

THE HUNGRY YEARS

Young Jack Dempsey —
a rising star within the heavyweight division.

Bernie helped Jack land a job as a mucker in a copper mine at the Ohio Copper Mine in Bingham Canyon, Utah. Jack was only sixteen years old. There were three types of miners in those days. There were the machine men. They were responsible for breaking out the ore. They generally earned around six dollars a day. Then there were the timber men. They were responsible for bracing the drifts with timber in order to decrease the chances of a cave-in. They were paid four dollars a day. The lowest mining position was that of the mucker. A mucker was paid approximately three dollars a day for loading small cars with ore and placing them in the shaft. The cars were then hoisted to ground level.

One day Jack was approached by a huge miner looking for a bit of amusement. The bully had a reputation for picking on men significantly smaller than himself. The miner threw dirt at the much smaller man. Jack warned the bully to stop picking on him. Sensing he may have found a perfect target, the bully repeatedly kicked more dirt at Jack. Dempsey warned the man to leave him alone. The bully laughed and promptly threw more dirt on the seemingly frightened victim. Jack lunged at the bully, swinging both fists at him. Jack immediately sensed the man had absolutely no boxing skills. The bully threw a right at his target, but Jack simply ducked under the wild swing and threw a vicious hard right at the bully's jaw, knocking him down and out.

Word quickly spread throughout the camp about Jack's victory. Miners eagerly congratulated him on his display of brute savagery. They shook Jack's hand and slapped him on the back. The bully was ridiculed for the beating he received from the much smaller Dempsey. Disheartened by all the ridicule he received from the other miners, the bully left the camp in disgrace.

Jack worked in the mines between fights over the next five years. Bernie and Jack, trying their hand at entrepreneurship, leased a mine situated in Cripple Creek, Colorado. The owner of the mine was promised 25 percent of any profits made. The pair worked day and night without the help of machinery. Ore was never found after months of backbreaking labor.

Jack had come to the conclusion that his own resolve to succeed was more important than any other factor. He was determined more than ever to become a champion in the pugilistic world. He realized he needed to seriously believe in himself because no one else would. Jack developed a hardened attitude toward his competitors in the ring.

Years later Dempsey reflected on his early boxing career. "Who knows how many fights I had between 1911 and 1916? The record books don't contain them, and I couldn't name the number or identify all the faces today if my life depended on doing it. I'd guess a hundred. But that's still a guess. Whatever the number was, it wasn't enough to support me. To fill the gaps and my belly, I was a dishwasher, a miner of anything you could dig up in Nevada, Utah, Colorado, and Idaho – I dug ditches, potatoes, and beets – punched cattle, shined shoes, and was a porter in the Hotel Utah in Salt Lake City."

Dempsey rode the rods in search of more opportunity. Up until now, the only opponents he could find were rank amateurs. He traveled all the way to Salt Lake City in search of fights. He worked as a porter in the Hotel Utah and received free room and board. Finally realizing there was practically no serious competition in Salt Lake City, he headed back to Colorado.

Riding the rods was an extremely dangerous mode of transportation. In order to escape detection, rod riders had to avoid riding inside the freight cars. They laid on top of rods that were located directly below the train cars. To avoid slipping off the rods, which would probably result in certain death, the rod riders had to tie their limbs to the lower rungs of the train…and pray.

Dempsey recalled years later just how grim and dangerous riding the rods actually was. "Most bums aren't steady enough to ride the rods, the two narrow steel beams beneath a Pullman. There's only a few inches between you and the tracks and roadbeds – and death. If you fall asleep, you'll roll off your narrow steel bed and die. If you're so cold you can't hold on any longer, you die. You can't ride too long without rest if it's rods you're riding on. There aren't any bells to ring to tell the man, 'Stop, kind sir, I want to get off.' You don't know how long it will be between stops. On warm nights you don't worry too much about that. But on winter nights in the mountain states, well, I often bet my life that the train would stop and let me off before I shook and shivered my way to my death beneath the wheels. You have to be desperate to gamble like that, but if you weren't desperate you wouldn't be on the rods."

Dempsey met many interesting characters in his travels, and he met more than his share of hobos, tramps, and bums. Dempsey explained that the hobo worked whenever the opportunity arose, and traveled to nowhere in particular. The tramp, on the other hand, refused to work and frequently traveled. Not to be outdone, the bum refused to work or travel altogether.

In Colorado, Dempsey tried a new tactic for getting fights. It was a method the great John L. Sullivan reportedly attempted to few takers because of his sheer size and intimidating stare. Dempsey would walk into a bar and announce in a painfully shrill, high-pitched voice that he could lick any man in the saloon. Jack only weighed around 130 pounds and looked like an easy target. In order to initiate some action, Dempsey passed his hat around. After money for the bets was collected, Dempsey proceeded to take on all comers. He invariably knocked each of his victims down and many of them out. There were times, however, when he recognized that he was vastly overmatched by a taker and he would wisely and speedily exit the bar.

Jack concluded that in order to make steady money fighting burley challengers in barrooms, he needed to keep moving on. His reputation for being a ferocious "giant killer" quickly spread throughout whatever region he happened to ply his trade. He eventually grew weary of the constant migration from one town to another. He needed to feel a sense of legitimacy in his life. Traveling from one back water town to another was demeaning at best.

Dempsey's earliest recorded fights occurred in 1914. He faced a fighter named Young Herman on August 18, 1914, at the Ramona Athletic Club Arena in Colorado Springs, Colorado. The outcome of the fight was officially declared a draw after six rounds. On November 30, 1914, Jack faced Billy Murphy at the Garrick Theater in Salt Lake City, Utah. He knocked Murphy out in the first round. On January 1, 1915, in Salt Lake City, Jack faced a fighter named Battling Jim Johnson. He knocked the hapless Johnson out in the first round.

About a month later in Utah, Dempsey took on Joe Lyons. He won by a knockout in the ninth round. On February 26, 1915, he fought Laverne Collier in Pocatello, Idaho. The fight was declared a draw after four rounds of action. On March 3, 1915, in Utah, he knocked out John Pierson in the seventh round. On April 1, 1915, in Utah, he knocked out Chief Gordon in the sixth round.

Jack hired several managers during this period. He never stayed with any manager for very long. This was probably due to the fact that Dempsey was only able to meet inexperienced managers in his travels. He was regarded as extraordinarily tough but inexperienced. The prospect of working with a successful manager who dealt only with experienced fighters was therefore very slim.

Dempsey fought all comers, even men much bigger and stronger than himself. Many of his opponents worked in the mining camps. He became so accustomed to fighting in the camps, he decided to once again try his hand at mining. Jack toiled deep in the bowels of the mines. His work area had practically no ventilation. Every day he moved heavy loads of ore and swung a pick to near exhaustion.

Jack's reputation as a fighter grew quickly. His reputation was so great, his foreman told him he was wasting his time working in the mines. He advised him to seriously pursue a career in boxing. Jack agreed with this sentiment and so he left the mines for good to pursue his true passion, knocking out grown men for a living.

In his autobiography, *Dempsey,* Jack explained how much mining meant to him in terms of how it affected his boxing career. "I fought just about anyone who was willing. I was so eager to obtain fights that I even fought out of my class, challenging rough miners from the mining camps around the area. I fought so many miners and went down into the shafts so often that I got a hankering for mining all over again. So back I went to doing the hard, dirty work no one else wanted. Lifting, hauling, moving a heavy load, wielding a pick, hour after hour with no sun, no adequate ventilation. I would wait and work as much as I'd have to and as much as I humanly could."

Jack met a wrestling promoter by the name of Otto Floto. Floto signed up Jack to fight miners. The caveat was that he had to fight them in one night. Jack earned several hundred dollars, but he paid a heavy price for it. After fighting one huge miner after another, Jack was exhausted and badly bruised. Later that same day, Floto and Dempsey were robbed by four mounted masked men.

Jack traveled to Salt Lake City in search of legitimate fights. He approached a man named Hardy Downing, a fight promoter who ran a boxing club. Dempsey convinced Downing that he was an up and coming heavyweight who could hold his own against almost anyone. Downing reluctantly agreed to add him to his roster of fighters for upcoming bouts.

At this time, Dempsey went by the name of Kid Blackie. Downing matched him up against a fighter named Kid Hancock. As soon as Jack entered the ring, the crowd booed and hissed at him. He promptly destroyed Kid Hancock in twelve seconds of the first round. Dempsey was beginning to prove just how lethal and ferocious he could be in the ring.

After the fight, Dempsey asked Downing for the five dollars he was promised. The promoter handed him two and a half dollars. Furious, Jack demanded the entire five dollars. The promoter explained that because Jack put his opponent's lights out quickly, the crowd was cheated out of a longer fight with more action. Downing convinced Jack that in order to receive the entire amount, he needed to fight Kid Hancock's brother. This time the crowd cheered for Kid Blackie while he demolished his opponent.

Dempsey's next fight was against a fighter named Jack Downey. The fight took place on April 5, 1915, at the Garrick Theater in Salt Lake City, Utah. Downey was a cigar maker and salesman by trade. Jack recalled that he "had a shiny, bald head and looked mean." Dempsey was amazed how good Downey actually was in the ring. Downey managed to block most of Jack's punches and he won the decision after the fourth and final round. Jack was thoroughly exhausted after the fight. He fully agreed that Downey was indeed the better fighter. The pair fought to a draw in their next bout.

Dempsey traveled to Reno, Nevada in search of more opportunity. He found a fighter by the name of Anamas (aka Emmanuel) Campbell. According to Jack, Campbell resembled Jack Johnson a great deal. Dempsey's reputation must have followed him because Campbell asked him to spar first in order to determine if Jack could be beaten. Dempsey deliberately looked bad during his sparring sessions with Campbell because he desperately needed a fight in order to eat. Convinced he could beat Jack, Campbell agreed to fight him.

The two fighters met on April 26, 1915, at the Jockey

Athletic Club in Reno, Nevada. Jack easily disposed of his opponent in short order. He won by a technical knockout in the fourth round. According to Dempsey, Campbell rose to his feet and told onlookers that Jack had tried to fool him in the gym and that he should never have fought Dempsey.

On May 31, 1915, Jack faced Johnny Sudenberg in Goldfield, Nevada. The fight was declared a draw after six grueling rounds. A few days later he faced Sudenberg again, this time in Tonopah, Nevada. Jack recalled that he knocked Sudenberg down several times in the first round. Sudenberg recovered enough to knock Jack down three times in the seventh round. The fight was declared a draw after ten bruising rounds of action. Reportedly, Dempsey and Sudenberg were each paid $100.

The two fighters found the nearest bar and drank beer in celebration of their hard-fought battle. Two thugs robbed them and everyone else in the bar. Broke and depressed, the pair borrowed a handcar and hand-pumped their way to a hole-in-the-wall town called Miner Junction. They strode into a saloon and announced to the patrons that they were professional fighters and were willing to fight each other for change. A hat was passed around the bar and the two battled each other for ten rounds. They earned $3.60 for their efforts.

Dempsey traveled to Montrose, Colorado, and met up with Fred Woods, a former school mate. They decided to promote a boxing match during Fair Week. Woods was a fight promoter's dream. He was built much bigger than Dempsey. Woods publicized the fight while Dempsey managed the event.

Jack prepared for the fight in an old wooden shed

located behind a blacksmith shop because he didn't want anyone to watch him train. He was still very sensitive about his scrawniness. He devised a new boxing tactic that later became one of his hallmarks. He taught himself to fight out of a low crouch while bobbing and weaving. This effective and aggressive tactic made him a difficult target to hit. Even a great fighter can be knocked out with a "lucky" punch and so Dempsey attempted to lessen that possibility.

On August 1, 1915, Dempsey faced Fred Woods at the Moose Hall in Montrose, Colorado. The gate receipts totaled a respectable forty dollars, not bad for two relatively unknown fighters. Dempsey knocked Woods out in the fourth round. Woods lay unconscious on the canvas for some time. Jack revived Woods by pouring ice water over his friend's face. After the fight, Dempsey and Woods removed all of the chairs to make room for the evening's festivities of dancing and music.

On October 7, 1915, Jack faced Andy Malloy at the Gem Theater in Durango, Colorado. He won a ten-round decision. Dempsey fought Malloy again on October 23 at the Moose Hall in Montrose, Colorado. This time Jack annihilated his opponent, knocking him out in the third round. After having been knocked out by Dempsey, Malloy saw a silver lining in his defeat. He offered to manage the victor and Jack readily agreed.

Malloy taught Jack some invaluable boxing lessons. He convinced his pupil that the entire body needed to be utilized, not just a fighter's fists. Dempsey appreciated everything Malloy had to offer him. In the end, however, the fight purses were hardly worth splitting between the partners. They decided to end their contract and go their separate ways.

Bernie reached out to Jack to let him know he had a fight lined up for him. Bernie had originally agreed to fight a tough miner named George Copelin, but he backed out of the deal. Jack was hesitant at first, but he finally agreed to let his brother off the hook. Jack thought that Bernie probably believed he was somewhat over the hill. And a loss to Copelin in front of his co-workers would be devastating to him.

Bernie warned Jack that Copelin was one of the best ore shovelers in the region. Jack reasoned that Copelin must be extraordinarily strong, a good quality for a fighter. A fifty-dollar award would go to the winner of the match. Bernie confidently bet on his younger brother to win.

Jack was adversely affected by the high altitude at Cripple Creek. He felt extremely exhausted most of the time, but Bernie made him train hard for the fight. Bernie insisted that Jack should drop his fight name, Kid Blackie, and replace it with the name, Jack Dempsey. Jack readily agreed.

Dempsey and Copelin did battle on November 19, 1915, at the Lyric Opera House in Cripple Creek, Colorado. When Jack entered the ring, the crowd booed and jeered him relentlessly. The spectators didn't recognize the skinny, undernourished kid wearing the white trunks. They had been bamboozled and they justifiably wanted their money back immediately.

The promoter, livid with rage, wanted to strangle Jack.

"Who the hell are you and where's Jack Dempsey?" the promoter screamed.

"I'm Jack Dempsey, sir," Jack sheepishly replied.

It was too late to call the fight off because the opening

bell had just sounded. Jack fought as valiantly as he possibly could, but the high altitude weakened his resolve. He tired fast. Jack later recalled there were two things that kept him competitive in this fight. He had gained a great deal of practical experience from previous fights. Secondly, the glory of winning in front of highly excited spectators and fans and the financial reward that goes with winning was another important element.

In the second round, Jack floored his opponent. Copelin quickly recovered from the knockdown and attacked Dempsey with a vengeance. By the third round, Dempsey began to tire. At the end of the fifth round, Jack warned Bernie that he had had enough. He was simply too exhausted to fight any further. Bernie convinced Jack that Copelin was about to collapse.

"He's as dead as you are," Bernie screamed at Jack. "Rush him!"

Jack was able to score a technical knockout in the sixth round against a very tough opponent. He could barely make it to his corner without help. As bad as Jack felt, Copelin looked and felt a lot worse. Bernie and Jack tried to collect additional money based on bets they had placed before the fight. The promoter informed the brothers that he had no money to give them. Dempsey became very discouraged with the fight game and all the unscrupulous characters it attracted.

Although he had won, Dempsey was deeply distraught about his performance in the ring. He thought his victory over Copelin was hollow. He had given all he could in order to convincingly beat his opponent, but Copelin simply would not go down and stay down. Jack had thought he was a much better fighter than Copelin before the match. But now his self-confidence had been shaken. In fact, Jack even seriously considered giving up boxing as a career.

Dempsey slowly but surely regained his confidence. On December 20, 1915, he scored a technical knockout over Jack Gillian at the Manhattan Athletic Club in Salt Lake City, Utah. Dempsey was beginning to take boxing seriously again.

Jack fought Johnny Sudenberg on February 1, 1916, at the Bijo Hall in Ely, Nevada. He destroyed his old nemesis by knocking him out in the second round. On February 21, 1916, Dempsey faced Jack Downey at the Manhattan Athletic Club in Salt Lake City, Utah. He knocked out Downey in the second round.

On February 23, 1916, at the Armory in Ogden, Utah, Dempsey fought a fighter who went by the name of the Boston Bearcat. It was rumored that this fighter once fought the great Sam Langford. What was especially impressive about Bearcat was the claim that he supposedly had never been knocked down by Langford. Bearcat claimed he was still on his feet after 20 grueling rounds with a fighter even the incomparable Jack Johnson feared. The Boston Bearcat, proud of his physique, allowed strangers to feel how solid his arms and stomach muscles were.

Dempsey was impressed with his opponent's physical attributes as the Bearcat stepped into the ring. At the beginning of the first round, Jack came out of his corner in a deep crouch and immediately attacked his opponent's mid-section. He continued to fight out of a crouch as he hammered away at his opponent with devastating blows to the head and mid-section. No longer able to withstand so much punishment, the Boston Bearcat dropped to the canvas in excruciating agony. He yelled to the referee to stop the count. He had received enough torment. The fight was declared over.

Spurred on by his latest victory, Dempsey trained harder than ever. He ran several miles each morning in order to increase his stamina. He experimented with different fighting techniques other boxers used over the years. He learned to charge his opponent while bobbing his head up and down, thus making him harder to hit.

Dempsey recalled that one of his greatest assets was his passion for boxing. He sincerely believed that in order for a pugilist to become a champion, he needed to love the sport of boxing. It wasn't enough to be merely talented, one needed to be passionate and hungry. Jack once related, "I was exceedingly lucky in sincerely loving the game. Not only the excitement and the applause, the anticipation of victory and the satisfaction of winning; I loved the actual give-and-take in the ring — the spur of competition, the zest of tremendous effort, the pride of being able to stand up under a stiff punch, the elation of feeling that on both the receiving and throwing end I was equal to my opponent, or even better than he was."

Jack was well received by boxers and managers alike. He asked them questions in order to improve his fighting skills and they responded with helpful suggestions, partially because he was so likable and easy to get along with. Jack listened intently to each suggestion and incorporated them into his own style of boxing. He experimented with all the tactics and strategies and utilized whatever method best fit his style of fighting. He concluded early on that self-education would continue throughout his entire career. Because he learned each opponent he faced had unique boxing skills and styles, Jack needed to adapt quickly in the ring in order to defeat his opponents.

Dempsey learned quickly from his mistakes in the ring. In his earliest fights, he threw wild punches instead of directing his blows at specific targets. He learned how dangerous it was to throw a punch and miss because of the fact that a fighter opens himself up to a counter-punch that could end the fight. A boxer also expends a lot more energy when he misses with a wild punch than when he successfully lands a punch. Dempsey learned it was vitally important to allow the other fighter to miss wildly as he ducked and weaved, waiting for the opportune moment to strike with savage force.

Jack was not afraid to take on opponents much bigger and taller than himself. He learned to use their apparent size and strength to his advantage. He learned to attack out of a low crouch while bobbing and weaving. This tactic allowed him to "come in under their best blows and hit up." He noticed that fighters who were exceedingly overweight and fighters who were lean and gangly were exceptionally prone to getting hurt from body blows to the stomach or as the boxing world called it, the "solar plexus."

On March 9, 1916, at the Mozart Theatre in Provo, Utah, Dempsey knocked out Cyril Kohen in the fourth round. Two scouts from Utah made a deal with Jack to fight a boxer named George Christian. The fight was held on March 17, 1916, at the Elko Theater in Price, Utah. According to Jack, Christian seemed quite confident he could easily beat the young, skinny Dempsey. He was sadly misinformed. Jack easily knocked out the overconfident Christian in one round. The downside to this incredible victory was the fact that Jack now found it exceedingly difficult to find a worthy opponent in and around Salt Lake City. It was time to move on to supposedly greener pastures.

Dempsey's next fight was held at the Bijo Hall on April 8, 1916, in Ely, Nevada. Ely was primarily known as a copper-mine town. His opponent was a Texan named Joe Bonds. Jack regarded Bonds as a very worthy opponent, perhaps his best to date. Bonds' previous manager was none other than Jack "Doc" Kearns, a man who would later play an extremely important role in Dempsey's boxing career. Bonds had distinguished himself by having attended the University of Puget Sound. He had also lettered in four sports, one of which was boxing.

Jack was well aware of Bonds' reputation as an exceptionally talented fighter. He was sure Bonds had never heard of him because when the two fighters were introduced to each other, Bonds gave Jack a "filthy look." Dempsey was of the opinion that Joe felt he could obliterate him in the ring.

Both fighters gave it their all. Jack recalled the bout was a "hard, fairly even ten-round battle." Bonds proved to be extremely difficult to hit. Jack stalked Bonds relentlessly, landing sharp blows to his opponent's head and mid-section. Dempsey won the decision after ten exciting rounds.

On May 3, 1916, at the Alhambra Theater in Ogden, Salt Lake City, Dempsey faced a fighter named Terry Kellar. Kellar had won several fights by the time he faced Dempsey. Jack won a hard-fought ten-round decision against his opponent.

On May 17, 1916, in Provo, Utah, Dempsey knocked

out Dan Ketchell in the third round. A few days later at the Elko Theater in Price, Utah, Jack knocked out Bob York in the fourth round. The fight was fairly even in the first three rounds. But then in the fourth round, Dempsey saw an opening and threw a hard left hook at York's jaw as he was moving forward. York hit the canvas and was counted out.

Jack decided now was the time to head east, particularly to places like New York City. In search of a new manager, he approached Hardy Downing and asked him if he knew anyone interested in managing an up and coming fighter such as himself. Downing advised him that Jack Price might be his best bet. Price agreed to manage Dempsey and he liked the idea of moving to New York. Jack described Price as a "big-hearted, fat, good-natured fellow who had a secret ambition of becoming a great dancer."

Dempsey had made enough money so that he could ride inside the train instead of under it. The pair had planned to pay their way to New York by finding fights along the way. There were no fights to be had in Grand Junction, Denver or Kansas City. Dempsey grew concerned about how difficult it might be to find work in New York if he couldn't find work in cities where people may have heard of him. Nevertheless, they pressed on to their ultimate destination.

Price and Dempsey arrived in New York City on a sweltering summer day. They carried less than thirty dollars between the two of them. Price proudly sported a ten-gallon hat and Jack desperately needed a shave and a shower. They were standing at the corner of Forty-second Street and Broadway when Jack approached a policeman. He asked the officer where he could find the "Great White

Way." The policeman laughed at Dempsey and told him he was standing in it.

Jack approached all the sports editors and proudly informed them who he was. They were not impressed at all with his boxing record. It began to dawn on Dempsey that because he was from the West, the New York City sports establishment probably never heard of him.

Jim Price, sportswriter for the *New York Press,* and Alfred Damon Runyon showed some interest in him. Runyon reportedly became the first sportswriter to use the name "Manassa Mauler" when referring to Dempsey. Jack Price made arrangements for Dempsey to be interviewed by Nat Fleischer. Fleischer would later become a highly respected authority on boxing. Runyon advised Jack to tough it out in New York. He advised Jack not to complain to anyone about his troubles because nobody really cared.

Most sportswriters strongly advised Dempsey to go back home. He was a complete nobody in New York. They didn't care about the newspaper clippings he carried with him. He may have knocked out twenty-six opponents, but nobody in New York had ever heard of them or cared to learn about them. Jack discovered that many fighters in New York were willing to fight for free just to get recognized by a fight manager or sportswriter. No one had ever heard of the Boston Bearcat, Johnny Sudenberg, or Bob York. Dempsey received more than his share of blank stares and ridicule.

Jack spent much of his time at Grupp's Gym which was located at 116th Street and Eighth Avenue. He learned how to throw hard and effective left hooks off of a left jab. This tactic would become one of his favorite weapons as fight fans and opponents would soon discover.

It was around this period when the name Jack Dempsey became his official fight name. Only close friends and family members called Dempsey "Harry." Some sportswriters referred to him as "Manassa Jack." The nickname that stuck, however, was the "Manassa Mauler." And for good reason. It sounded threatening and therefore it made for very good press.

Jack seemed to always be on the verge of starvation. He knew he needed to eat in order to keep up his strength while training. He learned saloons typically provided "free" food to any patron who bought beer at their establishment. Out of desperation, Jack sometimes purchased a nickel beer in order to be eligible to eat whatever was being offered at the bar. While Dempsey devoured his food, he quickly stuffed food down his pockets without the bartender noticing the infraction. By this method, Jack was able to gain badly needed weight.

Price finally found a fighter willing to do battle with Jack. The fight was scheduled to take place on June 24, 1916, at Billy Gibson's Fairmont Athletic Club at 149th Street and Third Avenue. Billy Gibson later became Gene Tunney's manager. Dempsey's opponent was Andre "Agile" Anderson, a former lumberjack who hailed from Chicago. He was a gigantic man. It seemed no one was willing to get into the ring with him. Jack weighed 173 pounds, forty-two pounds lighter than his opponent. Boxing experts praised Anderson as a formidable boxer who was well on his way to becoming a top-notch heavyweight contender. The fight was almost called off when the promoter saw how much smaller Jack was compared to the behemoth

Anderson. Billy Gibson warned Price that he would probably end up serving prison time for allowing his fighter to be murdered in the ring.

In the first round, Anderson pummeled Jack with blows so brutal, they sent him to the canvas several times. Dempsey returned to his corner "with gore smeared over his face." He took such a beating, the ring officials argued as to whether or not the bout should be halted. Anderson began to tire by the fifth round. In the tenth round, Anderson tried his best to dodge Dempsey's onslaught. Anderson frantically tried to cover up in order to evade Dempsey's attack. The fight was officially declared a "no decision" after 10 rounds. Nevertheless, Jack was declared the winner by sportswriters who witnessed the match.

The betting public by and large based the result of the fight on the consensus of the sportswriters. Damon Runyon praised Dempsey for his impressive boxing abilities and wished him luck in finding the right manager and trainer. Runyon wrote: "This lad from the West looks like promising material. With the right training and management, he may develop into a top-notcher." Dempsey's frailness prompted one writer to claim that Jack could use a meal. Unfortunately, he was paid just a few dollars for the fight.

New York sportswriters respected Dempsey because of his aggressive fighting style. He stalked opponents relentlessly around the ring as he pounded them with ferocious left hooks and hard rights to the face and body. He was known as a fearless "swarmer" in the ring. He constantly applied pressure on each opponent, relentlessly stalking and creating openings so he could unleash a maddening barrage of blows. Sportswriters enjoyed seeing only one fighter standing as the other boxer lay on the canvas in complete and utter agony. Dempsey was fast becoming a favorite among the New York press men, and more importantly, New York fight fans.

Jack learned that in order to land a hard punch, several factors had to come into play. A punch was most effective as an opponent moved forward, thereby absorbing the full impact of a blow. Dempsey discovered this tactic was not easy to implement because fighters moved so quickly in the ring and one needed to react as soon as possible in order to take advantage of a sudden and unexpected opening. Just as important, Jack learned, was the ability to protect oneself from being hammered. Dempsey learned that you "have to pull back or turn, to roll with the punch, in order to take the sting out of your opponent's blows."

In Dempsey's book, *Round By Round,* he explained in detail how he was able to get the most out of his style of attack. "The force of a blow," he carefully explained, "depends largely on the weight and momentum of the body behind it. As you strike with your right fist, your right shoulder has to come forward behind the blow to give it power, and the left shoulder swinging back at the same time helps turn your body and put even more punch into your right. You're then in a position to hit with your left, swinging your right shoulder back to get added force as your left fist comes forward. Consequently, weaving from side to side made me harder to hit, and at the same time gave me a two-fisted attack that alternated fast and powerful right and left blows. It was a development of what Andy Malloy had showed long before, of pivoting at the waist to increase the power of a punch."

Jack learned many tricks of the trade from fighters and managers. Some of his ring tactics were as simple as resting during the last ten or so seconds of a round near one's corner so that when the round ended, a fighter didn't have far to walk, thereby saving precious energy. This tactic, as Jack recognized, was not useful in a close fight. Viciously attacking one's opponent near the end of a round might very well sway the judges to rule in favor of the attacker.

On July 8, 1916, Dempsey faced William "Wild Bert" Kenny at the Fairmont Athletic Club in the Bronx, New York. Dempsey put on a respectable showing, flooring Kenny twice during the ten-round bout. The fight was officially declared a no decision. Sportswriters who witnessed the battle declared Dempsey the clear winner. Dempsey was paid a measly sum of money for his efforts.

Jack Price received word from Salt Lake City that his mother was terribly ill. Price immediately set out to see his mother, leaving Jack alone in New York. Dempsey now had neither money or friends. Soon after Price departed New York, a man known as John "the Barber" Reisler approached Dempsey. He claimed Price had sold him his contract with Dempsey. Jack couldn't believe the news at first. Reisler also insisted Price had borrowed fifty dollars against Jack's next bout. Dempsey insisted he never had a contract with Price.

"Sorry, kid," Reisler replied. "A deal's a deal. Here's some dough. Go out and buy yourself some decent clothes. You look like a goddamn bum!"

"He got his name from the big barbershop he owned on Broadway," Dempsey recalled later. "He was a gambler principally, but he liked to strut around the fight game.

I'll never know how he did it, but he became manager and business adviser to one of the greatest of them all, Sam Langford. Years later Al Laney of the *New York Herald Tribune* found Langford blind and starving in a Boston cellar, which could give you some idea of how John the Barber managed his affairs."

Dempsey tried to reason with Reisler, but the latter stood his ground. He was going to manage Dempsey and that was the end of it. Reisler shocked Dempsey by telling him his next opponent would be Sam Langford. Dempsey thought Langford could probably beat him to death in the ring. He thought he was too green to go up against such a seasoned professional as Langford. Reisler then suggested he should fight Gunboat Smith. Dempsey wisely told Reisler that Smith was also too experienced. He wanted some tune up fights before taking on such highly respected heavyweights.

Reisler grew furious and threatened to ruin Dempsey's career if he didn't fight John Lester Johnson. Dempsey reluctantly agreed. The fight was held on July 14, 1916, at the Harlem Sporting Club at 135th Street in New York. Reisler promised Jack he would receive 25 percent of the gate. Reisler claimed Jack's earnings would come to about five-hundred dollars. Dempsey thought he had finally hit the big time.

Johnson was a formidable and ferocious fighter. His punches felt like sledgehammers as they rained upon Dempsey's body. In the second round, Jack was hit so hard he doubled over in agony. He thought his ribs might have been broken. After the fight, the sportswriters were unsure exactly who won. In any event Dempsey felt proud of himself for slugging it out with such a brutal competitor. He confessed the pain caused by his broken ribs felt like he "was being stabbed with a sharp knife."

Dempsey decided to take it easy for a while so he could recuperate from the harsh thrashing he had received from Johnson. He was also extremely upset at Reisler for knowingly overmatching him against such a formidable adversary. Reisler reportedly paid Jack 100 dollars for his efforts.

"What about the gate receipts?" Dempsey screamed.

"What about them?" Reisler barked back. "Listen, you get what I pay you and let this be understood once and for all. Am I making myself clear?"

Jack was taken aback by Reisler's audacity and total lack of respect for him as a courageous young fighter. He explained to Reisler he needed time to heal. Reisler ignored Jack's complaints and continued to belittle him. Reisler noticed that Dempsey was indeed in bad shape. He told him to rest up but he also warned him to return for more fights. Dempsey reluctantly agreed. He was deeply depressed about his lack of success in the big city. His hopes and aspirations about finally making a respectable name for himself in the turbulent and dangerous business of boxing were dashed. Like his father before him, rightly or wrongly, he fled the scene of misery and failure. He needed to return to a part of the country where he was at least familiar with in order to begin anew. A fresh start is all he wanted at this point in his career.

Jack went back to Salt Lake City to see some old friends. He visited a woman named Maxine Cates whom he had previously met. Maxine worked as a prostitute in the red-light district on Commercial Street. She was a good fifteen years older than Dempsey and seemed to know her way around. She occasionally worked as a saloon piano player. Maxine began dropping hints about the two of them getting married. Jack had a hard time determining what she ever saw in him.

Jack and Maxine were finally married by a justice of the peace on October 9, 1916, in Farmington, Utah. The couple spent their honeymoon in a run-down hotel. Shortly thereafter, Jack began to realize that Maxine suffered from mood swings. He learned to bear the brunt of her hostility.

In order to get back into shape, Jack worked in the mines and even tried his hand at lumberjacking. As soon as his health improved, he returned to New York City. Reisler told Dempsey his next opponent would be Gunboat Smith. Jack complained once again he was not ready to challenge Smith in the ring. He wanted tune-up fights first before facing superior boxers.

Sensing Jack was deadly serious about not facing top talent at this stage in his career, Reisler suggested he fight Frank Moran. According to Dempsey, Moran was an even bigger threat than Gunboat Smith. When Jack told him he would not fight Moran under any circumstances, Reisler grew furious.

"Either fight this guy," Reisler threatened, "or get out of town. If you don't fight, I'll make it impossible for you to fight in this town — or for that matter any goddamn place else!"

Dempsey left New York and headed to Philadelphia where he hoped he would have better luck. He received the same treatment he experienced in New York. Sportswriters and promoters were unmoved by his ring history. Dempsey feared Reisler may very well have tried to ruin his reputation.

Disheartened, Jack traveled to Kansas City for a chance to fight anyone. Dempsey had heard that Frank Moran was training for an upcoming bout with Carl Morris. He visited Moran's training camp and asked if Moran needed a new sparring partner. Moran's people laughed Jack out of the camp. He decided to pay a visit to Morris' training camp to see if they could use him for sparring with big Carl Morris. Morris was six feet four inches tall and weighed 235 pounds. Despite the size differential, Jack was hired. He was paid seventy-five cents a day.

Morris gave Jack a hard time. To make matters worse, the fight between Moran and Morris was called off. It was rumored both fighters could not afford to lose a fight because they might miss the opportunity of fighting Jess Willard for the heavyweight title.

Jack traveled to Salt Lake City to reacquaint himself with his wife and to get some fights under his belt. Maxine complained to him that he needed to provide more support for her. The meager savings he sent her were not nearly enough for her to survive on. But there were other issues just as troubling. According to Jack, Maxine frequently sauntered in during the wee hours of the morning reeking of booze and cigarette smoke. Maxine's life style often led to more arguments and threats.

Dempsey's parents were not happy with his marriage to Maxine. His father had referred to her as a slut. His mother was appalled that Jack associated himself with a woman who plied her trade as a prostitute in a seedy part of town. For these reasons, Jack never allowed his wife anywhere near his parents.

Jack was determined more than ever to train seriously for upcoming bouts. He complained to Maxine that Salt Lake City was a dead end for him. He needed to go where the action was and he insisted that Maxine accompany him. She scoffed at his suggestion because she wanted to continue in her line of work. She refused to go along with him.

On September 28, 1916, at the Murray Fire Hall in Murray, Utah, Dempsey faced Young Hector. Jack desperately needed to end the fight quickly because his ribs were still healing from the battering he received from Johnson. He won by a technical knockout in the third round. On October 7, 1916, at the Biji Hall in Ely, Nevada, he fought Terry Kellar once again. He won a ten-round decision. On October 16, 1916, at the Salt Lake Theater in Salt Lake City, Jack won another ten-round decision against Dick Gilbert. A few days later in Salida, Colorado, Jack knocked Young Hector out in the second round.

Dempsey received word from promoter Fred Windsor about a possible upcoming bout. Windsor wanted Jack to face a boxer by the name of Fireman Jim Flynn. Dempsey had heard quite a bit about Flynn. Fireman Jim was a leading contender for the heavyweight title along with Bill Brennan, Carl Morris, Gunboat Smith, and Frank Moran. Jack immediately agreed to the arrangement even though he believed Flynn was a much better fighter.

The fight took place on February 13, 1917, at the Trocadero Hall in Murry, Utah in front of 400 spectators. In round one Flynn hammered away at Dempsey's body, knocking him down with a hard right to the head. Flynn continued to land hard blows at Jack's head and mid-section. Every time Dempsey rose to his feet, Flynn floored him with vicious rights and lefts. Sensing Jack might suffer from serious and perhaps permanent injury, Bernie threw in the towel. The knockout occurred approximately two minutes into the round.

Jack screamed at Bernie for ending the fight so quickly. Bernie tried to assure his brother there would be other fights and that this was not his night. Jack felt terrible about doubting his brother's decision. He feared another devastating blow from Flynn could end his career. But there was another side to the story regarding Dempsey's dismal performance.

Rumors quickly spread that Jack had thrown the fight for a good pay day. Dempsey later insisted his poor showing was due to a serious injury he experienced at a bowling alley where he worked. According to Jack, a co-worker accidently dropped a bowling ball on Dempsey's right hand. It was later alleged by Jack's manager at the time, Al Auerbach, that Jack took a dive because he desperately needed money.

Dempsey recalled much later that he had forgotten a basic rule in boxing. Until one is thoroughly warmed up, he wrote, "muscular action is not quite so rapid as it is after one has exercised freely and begun to perspire. Boxers meeting in the ring often feel each other out cautiously, dancing about, leading lightly, trying to gauge their opponent's ability and attack, warming up gradually. Often they are not quite so fast during the first few seconds of the fight as they are later on. Experienced boxers, knowing this, often will put in fifteen minutes or more of shadow-boxing in their dressing rooms before they enter the arena. Like

THE MILLION DOLLAR MAN

most young athletes, I didn't realize the importance of this thorough warming up before starting a fight."

Dempsey went on to explain further that "While I was still 'cold' with the first round less than a minute old, he landed his right on my jaw so hard that I went down like an ox. Only my youth and stamina enabled me to get back on my feet before the count of ten. Flynn had taken advantage of my inexperience by landing his bone-crusher during my initial attack so that my rush toward him gave added power to the blow. I had not been able to duck or side-step or pick the blow off. When I got to my feet I tried to cover up, but Flynn tore after me and down I went again. The blow wasn't so hard as the first one had been, since I wasn't rushing toward him when it landed, but it was hard enough. Down I went again. Twice more the same thing happened. After each knock down I got back on my feet just in time to catch another sock and go down again. Then, with nearly a minute of the round left to go, Bernie threw in the towel. I had lost by a first-round knockout."

Dempsey received word from Fred Windsor that he was interested in setting up another fight for him. In Seattle Jack trained in the local gyms and worked as a lumberjack. Windsor introduced Jack to Tommy Simpson's West Oakland Club. The club was situated in a very bad neighborhood in West Oakland, California. Because California law ruled bouts could not be longer than four rounds, fighters trained fast and furious. Each round counted a great deal and therefore a fighter had to prove himself every second in each of the four rounds. Dempsey's quick start in all his fights may very well be attributed to his training at the West Oakland Club.

Fred arranged for Jack to fight Al Norton at the West Oakland Club in Oakland, California on March 21, 1917. The fight was scheduled for four rounds and it would be the main event. The crowd cheered loudly for Norton, the local favorite. Dempsey received jeers and hisses. Dempsey bored in right after the opening bell, trading hard blows with his opponent. Norton proved to be a lot tougher than Jack had imagined. After the contest, the fight was officially declared a draw. An article on the fight in the *San Francisco Chronicle* begged to differ with the decision. "Dempsey looks to be a good boy," the *Chronicle* claimed, "and went through the four rounds unscratched." Norton, on the other hand, didn't fare as well. His battered face was evidence enough he had endured a terrible beating.

Dempsey's next fight was against Willie Meehan on March 28, 1917, in Emeryville, California. Meehan was fat but hard to punch. The fight was so boring to watch, several customers left before it had ended. Jack unexpectedly lost a close four-round decision to the vastly underrated Meehan.

On April 11, 1917, Dempsey fought Al Norton again at the West Oakland Club in Oakland, California. The fight was declared a draw after four rounds. Jack's reputation continued to suffer because of his embarrassing loss to Fireman Jim Flynn. He had difficulty finding decent paying fights. Windsor finally had to tell Jack he couldn't find any meaningful fights for him. Windsor wished Dempsey the best of luck and the two abruptly ended their partnership. Not able to make money boxing, Dempsey decided to look for work outside the fight world. He landed a job at the Tacoma Shipyards in Washington.

CHAPTER THREE

DESTINED FOR GREATNESS

Jack Dempsey and his manager Jack "Doc" Kearns.

O n a day that would prove critical to Dempsey's career, he wandered into a saloon not too far from the Oakland ferry. A woman approached Jack and asked him to buy her a drink. He told her he wasn't interested. Two patrons were arguing at one end of the bar. One of the men arguing was huge and the other was much smaller and well dressed. The two men started trading punches. The bigger man's friends joined in the fracas and began beating the smaller man unmercifully. At this point, Dempsey jumped in the middle of the fight and began punching the smaller man's attackers. Jack swung his fists in every direction, saving the smaller man from further injury.

The bartender yelled to everyone in the bar that he had just called the police. Fearing he might be arrested, Dempsey quickly walked out of the bar. Once outside, he overheard several people referring to someone named Jack Kearns. Evidently, several witnesses claimed Kearns had provoked the brawl. Jack seemed to remember his name in connection with the fighter Joe Bonds.

Years later Jack Kearns related the story about his first encounter with Dempsey. "I am in Al White's bar in Oakland that night," Kearns recalled. "I was just getting there, drinking myself into happy time. I am also having an argument with Dock Hansen, a middleweight I managed once. He is complaining because I didn't take him to Australia with me. He is beefing that he could lick Billy Murray, and Watson, another fighter I had on the trip, both in the same night. Pretty soon I am swinging blows with Hansen and one of his friends. They get me down and are ready to put boots to me. The next thing I know a young bruiser I never see before comes up, swinging both fists. Next the fight is all over and this dark-haired bruiser stiffened both Hansen and the other chump and cleaned out the joint."

"So I took to this young bruiser. He is tough-looking, unshaven gorilla, with jet-black hair, deep-set eyes. He also has high cheekbones, shaggy eyebrows, and his hair is scrambled in a short pompadour. I get talking to him and he says his name is Jack Dempsey."

Kearns introduced himself to Dempsey. "I'm Jack Kearns. You can handle yourself pretty good."

"The name's Dempsey," Jack told Kearns. "Jack Dempsey. I done some fighting under the name of 'Kid Blackie.'"

Kearns asked Jack where he was headed and Dempsey just shrugged. Jack explained he had just had a bad row with his wife. She had moved in with some friends and so he walked out. Kearns asked Jack if he would consider fighting for him. Dempsey expressed his deep disdain for the fight business. All he wanted at this point was a regular job.

Dempsey worked hard at the shipyard. Everything seemed to be going well for him until he received a wire from his mother. The message indicted that his brother Bruce had been viciously knifed while selling newspapers. He was only fifteen years old. Jack immediately rushed home to be with his dying brother. But it was too late. Bruce had succumbed to his wound and died. Dempsey's parents were devastated by Bruce's death. Jack pleaded with his father not to avenge the murder of his youngest son. The motive behind Bruce's unfortunate tragedy was never revealed to the family.

Jack had reached a low point in his life. He had nowhere to turn. He had no idea where his wife was and he lost his job at the shipyard. One day Dempsey received a letter from Jack Kearns, the man he had saved from a beating in Oakland. In the letter, Kearns stated that "it took a tough man to take on tough opponents and win." He also indicated he was very much interested in becoming Jack's manager. He wanted to know if Jack was still interested in returning to the ring. Jack was taken aback by Kearns' question. He had never quit boxing but his fights had been so minor and underreported, Kearns probably never learned about them.

Dempsey immediately sent a letter back to Kearns expressing his wholehearted acceptance to Kearns' offer. He indicated in his letter that he would fight anybody, anywhere, and anytime. Jack received another letter from Kearns. Enclosed in the envelope was a train ticket from Salt Lake City to San Francisco and a five-dollar bill. Jack was impressed with Kearns' professionalism. It was a far cry from the way John "the Barber" had treated him and he was grateful for it. Before he left, Jack tried to locate his wife. Not surprisingly, he couldn't track her down. He left her a note indicating she could flop at his parent's home if things got too desperate for her.

Jack finally arrived in San Francisco. He quickly jumped onto the train platform and looked around for Kearns. He had difficulty seeing through the cloud of steam emitting from the train. Suddenly, he heard someone call out his name. He spun around and noticed a small, neatly dressed man. The immaculately dressed stranger wore a vested suit and what appeared to be a diamond stickpin in his necktie. The man was none other than Jack Kearns.

Kearns was the exact antithesis of Dempsey in temperament. Curiously, they seemed to complement each other as well. Jack was unassuming, dressed very simply, and was soft spoken, almost shy. He rarely expressed his feelings to anyone. He may have assumed that no one really cared about what a mug like him had to say. Jack Kearns, on the other hand, was brash, a braggart, and well dressed. He was very condescending and insulting, even toward Dempsey. Jack sensed Kearns was the sort of man he needed as a manager. Kearns was someone who would be willing to cheat and lie in order to get the upper hand in an important deal.

Jack Kearns' real name was John Leo McKernan. He was born on August 17, 1882, in Waterloo, Michigan. His parents were very poor and so young Jack had to try and eke out a living on his own at an early age. He sometimes worked as a bouncer in run-down saloons located up and down San Francisco's infamous Barbary Coast.

Kearns' early life in many ways mirrored Dempsey's. They shared big dreams about making a name for themselves and they both left home at a very early age. "Tales of the gold mine my father, John Philip McKernan, owned in Montana were one of the great entertainments of my boyhood. He took $100,000 out of it, banked it, and the bankers absconded with it. He had better luck as a scout for General Custer. He quit just before Little Big Horn. The wanderlust I inherited from my father and those gold mining yarns undoubtedly account for the fact that at the age of fifteen I lit out for the Klondike, where gold had just been discovered. I had been born on a Michigan farm, grew to seven on a North Dakota ranch and then, with my father acting as scout, rode a wagon train to North Yakima in the new state of Washington. Along the way, and in other travels, I picked up more than a smattering of such languages as Sioux, Crow, Kiowa, Blackfoot, Comanche, Chinook – and Swedish."

McKernan worked as a ranch hand on the 79 Ranch, located a few miles from Billings, Montana. He must have been athletically inclined because he also tried out as a baseball player for a Seattle team that was associated with the Pacific Coast League. The manager of the ball club told McKernan that a decision as to whether or not he made the team would be forthcoming.

Apparently, McKernan had other ideas about becoming a baseball player because he began boxing for a living. He changed his name to Jack Kearns and initially fought in the lightweight division. His fight name was "Young Kid Kearns," a name that would not go down in the annals of boxing folklore. Eventually he fought as a welterweight. Kearns never really became a successful boxer and so after about sixty bouts be decided to quit fighting for a living. He summed up his career as a boxer by stating that "I was always a poor judge of distance in a fight. I never knew how long I was going to last or how far I was going to fall."

Aware that his career as a boxer was going nowhere fast, Kearns decided instead to try his hand at managing fighters. Making a living as either a fighter or manager in California was difficult. Because the state dictated a bout could not be longer than four rounds, purses were exceedingly low. At one point Kearns was reduced to managing a 250-pound wrestler named "Mystery Man."

By 1915 Kearns managed several fighters. His stable of boxers included heavyweight Joe Bonds, middleweights

"Fighting" Billy Murray and Jimmy Clabby, and light-weight Red Watson. In July 1915, Kearns and his fighters traveled to Australia for several boxing tournaments. His stable performed badly in the Land Down Under. As soon as they arrived back in the states, Kearns decided he had had his fill of managing and quit.

Dempsey needed Jack Kearns as much as Kearns needed Jack. Essentially, their careers had hit a road block and there was nothing promising on the horizon. Kearns was not having much luck successfully managing fight-ers and Jack was beginning to get the reputation of being "punched out." Jack seriously considered quitting the fight game in 1917. He had won many fights but he also received a lot of brutal beatings along the way. Without proper guidance, he was simply going nowhere fast in a very savage and unforgiving business.

What Kearns initially saw in young Dempsey was not overly promising. Jack was extremely skinny and often appeared exhausted. He was still feeling despondent about Bruce's murder. Kearns jumped into action immediately. He introduced Jack to his mother. Kearns' mother took a liking to Jack immediately and treated him like a son. She cooked for him and soon Jack began gaining much needed weight. Kearns explained to Jack that he needed to gain his strength back before he could train.

Kearns and Dempsey got along very well. Kearns revealed to Jack that his last name was actually McKernan. He was born in Michigan. His parents uprooted the family to Washington. He also had a sister, but never revealed any-thing about her. He ran away from home at the tender age of fourteen. His destination was the Klondike in Alaska.

He had held many unusual jobs, such as a cemetery plot salesman, and a gambler.

Jack spilled his guts to Kearns. He told him about his failed marriage to Maxine, his horrible loss to Fireman Jim Flynn, and his inability to find a manager who believed in his potential as a serious heavyweight contender. Dempsey earnestly listened to Kearns' badly needed pep talks. He discovered Jack Kearns was "a crafty alligator who connived for success, a man who would stop at nothing and would not be stopped."

Kearns built a gymnasium inside his house. He made Dempsey work out for several hours and into the early evening. Kearns arranged for one of his old-time fighters, Marty Farrell, to spar with Jack. Farrell showed Dempsey how to throw a left hook more effectively.

Kearns also arranged for Jack to spar with an experienced boxer named "Red" Watson, a rough and tough fighter who could inflict terrible damage with both hands. Kearns whispered to Watson that he wanted him to attack Jack with everything he had. Watson obliged and rushed Jack from the outset, hitting him with a vicious left hook that shook Dempsey to the core.

"Hey, take it easy," Dempsey warned the fighter. "I ain't had the gloves on for a long time."

"He's a big bum," Watson sneered. "I'll flatten him." Kearns encouraged Watson to attack Dempsey without mercy.

Watson pounded Jack with more hard blows to the face and body. Jack grew angry and turned into a raging tiger. Dempsey attacked Watson with devastating blows until Kearns stepped in and called for a time out. Dempsey proved to Kearns not only could he take a wallop, but he could turn into a ferocious fighting machine at any moment.

Convinced he had a diamond in the rough, Kearns immediately put Dempsey to work. He noticed Jack was "right-hand crazy" so he made him toss a baseball left-handed. After a while, Jack became comfortable throwing lefts without hesitating. He ordered Jack to snap his punches as quickly and as hard as possible while Dempsey held heavy weights in both hands.

Kearns, always the showman, allowed his friends to watch Dempsey work out and spar. Jack always felt very uneasy about strangers watching him train. Kearns explained to him this was his way of promoting Jack's abilities as a boxer. Sometimes word of mouth can be a very effective method of self-promotion.

One of Kearns' friends, a fight promoter, told him he was wasting his time taking on Dempsey.

"You must be kidding," the promoter warned him. "Why, he ain't worth two cents!"

"All he needs is a little time," Kearns retorted.

"Why don't you feed him? Maybe with a little weight he'd look like something."

Dempsey, who was present during the conversation, was livid. He wanted to put the man's lights out, but Kearns wisely restrained him. Kearns told the promoter he was planning on matching Jack against one of Dempsey's old rivals, Willie Meehan. The promoter scoffed at Kearns' suggestion.

The bout was held on March 28, 1917, in Emeryville, California, a town located near Oakland. Thousands of Meehan fans showed up at the four rounder. Although

Meehan won the decision, Kearns told Jack he was very pleased with his performance. Meehan turned out to be one of the few opponents Jack had trouble beating in the ring. Dempsey received $250 for his effort.

Kearns arranged for Dempsey to fight another of Jack's old rivals, Al Norton. The fight was declared a draw after four brutal rounds. On July 25, 1917, Jack faced Willie Meehan at the Arena in Emeryville, California. This time Jack won the decision in a hard fought four-rounder. It was becoming very clear to the boxing world that Dempsey's abilities were improving rapidly.

On August 1, 1917, in Emeryville, California, Dempsey took on Al Norton. Jack knocked Norton out in the first round. Two more fights against the crafty Meehan were declared four-round draws. On September 19, Dempsey fought Charley Miller in Emeryville. He won by a technical knockout in the first round. A few days later Jack fought another bout in Emeryville. He won a four-round decision against Bob McAllister, a highly respected heavyweight from the west coast. Fighters were beginning to realize Dempsey was extremely hard to beat.

Elated by Dempsey's fighting prowess, Kearns decided Jack was ready to take on Edward J. Smyth, or as he liked to be called, Gunboat Smith, the man Jack refused to fight not too long ago. The bout would be held in the Mission Baseball Park in San Francisco and it was scheduled for four rounds.

Gunboat Smith had actually been hailed as the "white" heavyweight champion of the world when on January 1, 1914, he beat Arthur Pelkey in Daly City, California. Six months later he lost the "title" to Georges Carpentier. Smith redeemed himself, however, when he defeated Jess Willard, the "Pottawatomie Giant" prior to the title fight in which Willard destroyed the great Jack Johnson in Havana, Cuba in 1915.

Dempsey had mixed feelings about his upcoming bout with Gunboat Smith. First of all, Smith had beaten Jess Willard in the ring. He also feared that if he lost to Smith, Kearns would drop him. On the other hand, if Jack won, his standing in the heavyweight division would rise dramatically. Kearns the gambler was obviously rolling the dice on Dempsey's chances.

Gunboat Smith had the reputation of being the best white heavyweight during a period known as the "Great White Hope" era. He had beaten several outstanding opponents such as Frank Moran, Jess Willard, and probably the most feared and dangerous of all the challengers for the heavyweight crown, Sam Langford. Even the great Jack Johnson was known to have ducked Langford on several occasions.

Dempsey felt fairly confident he could hold his own against Gunboat Smith. But he had reservations as well. He made Kearns promise not to throw in the towel under any circumstances. Kearns vowed he would not end the fight even under the most dangerous of circumstances. Dempsey was obviously proud of his recuperative powers. Memories of his battle with Fireman Jim Flynn still haunted him.

The bout was held on October 2, 1917, at the Mission Baseball Park in San Francisco. Jack was careful not to get too close to Smith. He was concerned his opponent might knock him out as Flynn had done. Early in the fight Smith smashed a hard right to Dempsey's chin. Jack was hurt but managed to keep fighting back. Kearns' and Jack's second, Spider Kelley, screamed at Dempsey to throw some punches at Smith.

"You've got him!" Kearns screamed at Dempsey. "Just keep away from him until you've softened him up! You're better than he is!"

In the second round, Gunboat Smith hit Dempsey with a ferocious blow that nearly ended the fight. Dempsey later claimed the punch was the hardest he had ever been hit with in his entire career up to that point. After the fight, Jack felt disgusted with himself. He had lost.

"I guess I'm no match for Gunboat," Jack said to Kearns. "I'm real sorry I let you down. I guess I'm not what you thought I was."

"Kid, you won!" Kearns blurted out. "Gunboat hit you with a right and I thought it'd kill you, but you nearly killed him!"

"I don't remember a thing," Dempsey told an incredulous Jack Kearns. "After he hit me in the second round, I thought he knocked me out." Kearns was impressed with Dempsey's unique ability to annihilate opponents while apparently fighting subconsciously. Kearns had never heard of a situation in which a boxer was capable of fighting while apparently "unconscious." He was convinced "we could go all the way." Of course, Jack had heard this same claim from countless other managers. This time, however, he believed his new manager because he respected Kearns' ability as a fight manager.

The fight essentially ended Gunboat Smith's chances of ever being a top-rated heavyweight contender. Dempsey learned an important lesson from that fight. He discovered he had been knocked out, but not in the conventional manner. Jack was able to continue fighting but only in an unconscious state. He firmly believed intensive training allowed him to fight Smith intuitively without consciously being aware of his surroundings.

Kearns wasted no time teaching Jack everything he knew about the fight game. He even taught him how to scowl and walk as a champion. "Keep those feet together and you can slide in under a punch and counter-punch," Kearns instructed Jack over and over again. Kearns hired Marty Farrell, a very effective middleweight, to show Jack how to punch more effectively out of a weave. These lessons vastly improved Dempsey's speed. His bobbing and weaving style enabled him to confuse much larger heavyweights.

Kearns told Jack his next fight would be against Carl Morris. Jack voiced his concerns to Kearns about facing Morris so early in his career. He reminded Kearns just how big and tough Morris was and that he thought it was a mistake to take him on. Kearns advised Dempsey he shouldn't have a problem with Morris. He assured him that the size of an opponent shouldn't matter. He calmly informed Jack that "the bigger they come, the harder they fall."

Dempsey faced Carl Morris, also known as the "Sapulpa Giant" at the Dreamland Pavilion in San Francisco on November 2, 1917. Jack was determined to beat Morris early in the fight. He never got over the feeling of being humiliated by Morris and wanted to avenge the way Morris had treated him. Although Dempsey weighed only 180 pounds to Morris' 235 pounds, Kearns was confident his fighter would prevail.

Carl Morris was the clear favorite to win the fight.

Among the many fans attending the fight were none other than Al Jolson, Rube Goldberg, and lawman Wyatt Earp. Kearns was convinced his promotional methods were finally paying off.

Dempsey's plan for the fight was to try and outbox Morris. But Jack noticed early in the first round that this strategy was worthless. Morris kept attacking Jack with hard blows to the face and body. Dempsey described Morris' fists as "battering-rams." All Jack could do in the face of Morris' onslaught was to grab and hold on to his opponent. He found this defensive tactic to be useless because Morris was able to wiggle his arm free and pound Dempsey. Jack felt certain Morris would be the clear winner in the fight.

In the second round, Dempsey finally figured out a way to fight Morris. As his opponent moved forward, Jack threw short, hard punches at Morris' midsection. Jack was also able to duck many of Morris' punches at close range.

In the third round, Morris changed his tactic from exchanging short-range blows with Jack to boxing. Jack continued to bore in as Morris tried to evade Dempsey's powerful left hooks and right-crosses. In the fourth and final round, Morris absorbed a lot of punishment from Dempsey. After the fight, Jack was declared the winner in a brutal battle between two very tough and formidable fighters.

After the fight, Kearns and Dempsey traveled to Denver. Kearns proudly informed H.H. Tammen of the *Denver Post* that in his very presence stood the future heavyweight champion of the world. Tammen, like so many other newspaper men, scoffed at Kearns' fighter. Tammen became even less impressed with Dempsey when he spoke to Tammen in his high-pitched voice. Tammen told the pair he was too busy to talk with them and asked them to leave.

Just as the pair exited the building, Kearns spotted Jess Willard, the heavyweight champion, walking alone in front of them. Kearns took full advantage of the opportunity fate had bestowed on him. He approached the giant Willard and tried to convince Jess to fight Dempsey for the title.

Willard was visibly annoyed by Kearns' attempt to force the champion into defending his title against a relatively unknown fighter. He informed Kearns he absolutely refused to fight during a world war. Kearns insinuated that Willard was only concerned about losing and for no other reason. He told the champ it was unfair of him to hog the title. Somehow Kearns made Willard promise to fight Jack first once he decided to defend the title.

Pressing his luck, Kearns rushed right back into the Denver Post building. He managed to corner Otto Floto and told him Willard had promised to fight Dempsey the first chance he got. Kearns added that the proceeds would go to a charity. Floto, excited by this exclusive, informed Kearns that this latest development would be printed in the newspapers as an extra. Kearns was ecstatic.

Kearns and Dempsey traveled to Chicago and hit all the newspaper offices. They soon ran out of money in the big city. It was winter and they desperately needed warmer coats. Kearns managed to borrow money from a promoter friend for the coats.

One day while sitting inside a hotel lobby, Kearns was accosted by an extremely aggravated Jess Willard.

"That was a cheap trick you pulled," Willard snarled

at him. "When I decide to fight again, it'll be with some-one who earned it."

Jack felt embarrassed by the scene and stepped away from the altercation. Everyone in the lobby was shocked at what they had just witnessed. Willard finally turned and walked out of the hotel, leaving Kearns completely speechless.

Kearns gathered his senses and proceeded to write a letter to Willard. In the letter, he expressed his revulsion about the champ refusing to fight Dempsey. After all, the proceeds would go to several worthwhile charities as well as to America's soldiers fighting in a foreign land. Jack tried to stop Kearns from sending the letter, but he was adamant. Kearns later learned that after reading his letter, Willard absolutely refused to meet Dempsey in the ring.

In an effort to get more publicity for Dempsey, Kearns arranged for a press conference. He announced to the sportswriters he was willing to bet ten thousand dol-lars Jack could lick any two fighters in one night. The press could even choose the fighters themselves. Dempsey was stunned at this revelation. They were both broke. Dempsey pleaded with Kearns not to go through with his offer.

"Don't you know that's the name of the game," Kearns explained. "Look, it's great publicity for us, and what's more, no person's got that kind of dough to lay out."

In was beginning to dawn on Dempsey that Kearns did in fact possess a unique talent. His promotional skills were brilliant and very effective. Kearns understood human nature and the power of promotion. Kearns told sto-ries about Dempsey's alleged savage temperament, super human strength, and bloodline to sports editors, writers, and promoters. Many newspapers were only too happy to print Kearns' sensational assertions. The readers were fascinated about Dempsey's apparent invincibility. Everyone, that is, except for Jess Willard.

Kearns did everything in his power to try and shame Willard into fighting Dempsey. Long before Muhammed Ali tried his highly successful campaign of baiting Charles "Sonny" Liston into facing him in the ring, Kearns had learned that "like a stripper you had to use exposure." Dempsey and Kearns were well aware of the fact that there existed many well qualified heavyweight challengers. Because of this fact, Kearns knew he needed to aggressively campaign for his fighter.

The genius of Jack "Doc" Kearns is reflected in the fact that since taking on Dempsey as his fight manager, he was able to move Dempsey up the ranks of the heavyweight division in a relatively short period of time. He was not only able to sharpen and improve Jack's skills as a fighter, but he was also able to sell Jack to the all-important and very influential news media, namely the sportswriters of America.

Many sports editors eagerly watched Dempsey's workouts in Kid Howard's gym. The editors, however, were not impressed with Jack's training sessions. Dempsey himself admitted he "never looked good working out." Perhaps he felt embarrassed in front of strangers as he shadow-boxed and hit the big bag.

Jack's next fight was against Kalamazoo native Homer Smith, a top contender. The fight was held on January 24, 1918, in Racine, Wisconsin. Dempsey's earnings totaled a mere $800. Floyd Fitzsimmons, Smith's manager and an old friend of Kearns, had set up the fight. Fitzsimmons apparently felt sorry for Kearns and gave him a shot out of pity. Homer Smith was able to hold his own against another top contender, Bill Brennan. His battle with Brennan was declared a draw.

Just as the opening bell sounded, Smith rushed toward Dempsey. He drove a right to Jack's head. Dempsey ducked under Smith's punch and landed a hard right to Smith's body. The sound of the blow could be heard clear across the arena. Dempsey then hammered away at Smith's midsection with everything he had. Smith lowered his guard to protect his midsection and Jack landed a hard left-hook to the side of Smith's head. Smith was counted out at 55 seconds of the first round.

Kearns began referring to Dempsey as "Jack the Giant Killer" and the "Man Eater." The public ate it up. Boxing fans had never seen a heavyweight boxer fight with such determination and urgency as Jack Dempsey. Before Jack arrived on the scene, most boxers stood straight up and demonstrated very little agility. Dempsey, on the other hand, moved like a fearless panther toward his opponent, eying his prey at first and then suddenly rushing in for the kill.

Whether they knew it or not, fight promoter Tex Rickard and Jack Kearns were in dire need of each other. Jess Willard had defended the title only once since knocking out Jack Johnson in 1915 in Havana, Cuba. He had fought Frank Moran in an utterly boring farce of an exhibition in March 1916. To Rickard's credit, the gate receipts totaled a very impressive $152,000. It represented the largest gate for an indoor sporting event. Willard stayed out of the ring for good after the exhibition.

Tex Rickard liked what he had heard about the

relatively unknown Jack Dempsey. He had heard that Jack was from the west and that he somehow reflected the wildness and brutality from that part of the country. Perhaps he may have read a stirring account regarding Dempsey's brutality by author Frank Graham, Jr. Young Jack's "broad-shouldered, slim-wasted torso, brakeman's haircut, and his dish nose," the author noted, established him as a "perfect fit for those stories about the young savage punching his way out of the West's hobo jungles to win the heavyweight championship of the world."

Novelist Joyce Carol Oates was fervently impressed with Dempsey's savagery as well. The author noted that the "swiftness of his attack, his disdain for strategies of defense, endeared him to greatly aroused crowds who had never seen anything quite like him before."

Tex Rickard actually promoted and even refereed the "Battle of the Century." Jim Jeffries had reluctantly come out of retirement and faced the world's heavyweight champion, Jack Johnson. Much of America was in an uproar over the fact that Jack Johnson, a black man, towered over all others in the heavyweight division, the most prestigious division in all of boxing. Johnson easily beat Jeffries in a thoroughly one-sided fight. Fully aware there were no legitimate "White Hopes," Rickard abandoned the fight game. He decided to try his hand at ranching and so he bought 5 million acres of land in Paraguay. He impressed the country's government officials by raising 50,000 head of cattle. Former President Theodore Roosevelt was also deeply impressed with Rickard's accomplishment and even referred to Tex as his "old Western friend."

For the first time, sportswriters began writing about

Dempsey's exploits in the ring. There were many, however, who scoffed at Dempsey's chances against Willard. Bat Masterson relentlessly attacked Dempsey as a fraud. He wrote that Dempsey "hadn't had a square fight in a year." Masterson appeared to be suffering from selective memory because he refused to own up to the fact that Willard had not fought a real fight since winning the title in 1915. When it was officially announced sometime later that Willard would fight Dempsey for the title in Toledo, Ohio, Masterson claimed Dempsey's fights were "setups and fakes" and that Jack would "be lucky to leave Toledo alive."

Kearns promptly contacted promoter Charlie Murray and told him that his fighter was willing to face Morris. Murray was unsure if Dempsey could go up against a giant like Morris. He mailed money for transportation costs to Kearns and Jack. He wanted to see Dempsey in person before making a final decision.

Kearns and Dempsey arrived in Buffalo in the middle of a blizzard. Thinking they could meet Murray first thing in the morning, the two stayed at the Hotel Iroquois for the night. Suddenly, there was a loud knock on the door. Murray entered the room and asked Kearns where Dempsey was. Jack approached Murray and introduced himself.

"Okay, Kearns," Murray snarled. "A joke's a joke. I know this kid's some middleweight you keep around. Now where's Dempsey?"

Kearns assured Murray that the fighter standing in front of him was indeed Jack the Giant Killer.

"What's the big idea?" Murray yelled. "You told me he was six feet two, weighing at least 230. This little guy doesn't even come near 190. I can't put him in the same ring with Morris. The public wouldn't stand for it!"

Feeling Murray's wrath, Kearns tried to assure him that Jack should face Morris. After all, Dempsey beat Morris in a four rounder. Murray was unconvinced. He told Kearns that Morris was tougher than he was when Dempsey beat him. Morris would crush Dempsey this time. The two men argued back and forth. Finally, Jack stepped in to defend himself.

"Mr. Murray, you've gotta let me go ahead with this fight. Tell you what. If I don't lick Morris, you can give my end of the purse to the poor kids in Buffalo. Listen, we need that dough. Please let me take him on. It means everything to me." Murray, moved by Dempsey's plea, agreed to go ahead with the match.

Kearns warned Dempsey that Morris had a reputation of being "one of the foulest fighters of all time." He told him he would be in the fight of his life and he needed to do whatever it took in order to beat Morris. That meant even if he had to resort to some of Morris' dirty tactics. Jack assured Kearns not to worry.

On February 4, 1918, at the Broadway Auditorium in Buffalo, New York, Dempsey and Morris slugged it out round after round. Dempsey had decided early on to move in close to Morris so he could land short-range bombs to the body. Morris proved to be a lot tougher than when Jack fought him the last time. Almost every time Dempsey landed a hard blow, Morris countered with a low blow. According to Kearns, Morris "thumbed, heeled, butted, hit low, and even used his knee" in order to win. Morris was warned several times by referee Dick Nugent. Finally, the referee stopped the fight and awarded the contest to Dempsey on a foul in the sixth round.

Kearns wired Fireman Jim Flynn a rather impressive guarantee to fight Jack. He reminded Flynn this was the same Jack Dempsey Flynn had defeated just a year earlier.

"I knocked this bum out in one round a year ago," Flynn informed his manager. "I'll do an even quicker job this time," he crowed.

On February 14, 1918, in Fort Sheridan, Illinois, Dempsey knocked out Jim Flynn inside one round. To many cynics, the result proved the theory that Jack had taken a dive during their previous match. Flynn admitted after the fight that he was utterly amazed at Dempsey's punching power. He joked that if Kearns ever wanted to quit the boxing world, he would gladly take his place managing Dempsey.

Kearns thought Jack was ready to take on Bill Brennan. Instead of pressuring Leo P. Flynn, Brennan's manager, to fight Dempsey, Kearns tried a new angle. He asked several influential sportswriters who they thought Jack should fight next. Whenever Brennan's name was mentioned as a viable opponent for Dempsey, Kearns agreed wholeheartedly with the suggestion. Sportswriters indicated in their columns that now was the time for Bill Brennan to face Dempsey. Feeling the pressure, Flynn finally agreed to allow his fighter to go up against Dempsey.

Jack thought very highly of Bill Brennan as a person and as fighter. He had always been grateful for Brennan's help while Jack was struggling to make a name for himself. Brennan was kind enough to hire Jack as a sparring partner when no one else would during Dempsey's first trip to New York. He made sure Jack had enough to eat and a place to flop.

Just before the fight, Brennan approached Jack in his

dressing room. The two fighters shook hands and then Brennan warned Dempsey he may have to hurt him in the ring. "That butcher you've got as a manager shouldn't have signed for this fight. I didn't want it, but that lousy publicity he put out about you forced me to take it. Jack, I'm gonna have to flatten you. I don't want to. You're coming along just great, and I'm sorry I've got to spoil it. But that big clown Fulton is ducking me. If I don't take you out big, Fulton will get that shot at Willard. So you gotta go. I hope you understand."

"Bill," Jack explained. "I'm no hungry bum no more. Don't worry about me. I'll knock you kicking in the first round."

Brennan laughed at Jack's apparent overconfidence. He slapped him on the back and wished him the best of luck.

The Dempsey-Brennan bout was held on February 25, 1918, at the Auditorium in Milwaukee, Wisconsin. Dempsey wanted to end the fight quickly and tried for a knockout in the first round. Jack rushed Brennan and hammered away at his head and midsection. Brennan dropped to the canvas. Brennan, glassy-eyed from the Dempsey onslaught, struggled to get to his feet. In the second round, Dempsey knocked Brennan to the canvas several times. In the sixth and final round, Jack hit Brennan hard, causing him to spin around. Just as Brennan crashed to the canvas, Jack heard a loud snap. Brennan had broken his ankle. Dempsey won by a technical knockout in the sixth round.

As Jack stepped out of the ring, he heard several people shout a word at him that made him sick. It was a word he would hear throughout the rest of his career. The word

Dempsey learned to dread was "Slacker."

The *New York Times* reported that "The Californian had a shift that Brennan seemed unable to fathom. Dempsey landed almost at will." Jack entered Brennan's dressing room to see how he was holding up. The two fighters spoke about the fight for a while and then when Jack turned to leave, Brennan called out to him.

"Next time you get dumped, Jack," Brennan said, smiling.

Shortly after the Brennan fight, Jack took on a fighter named Jack Smith on March 16, 1918, in Memphis. It was discovered after the fight that his real name was Fred Saddy or Fred Soddy. In either case, he knocked his opponent out in the first round. Saddy was reportedly a common sparring partner. Allegedly he went under the assumed name of Jack Smith for the fight in order to exaggerate the significance of a win for Dempsey if he was victorious. Kearns, of course, denied he knew anything about the apparent ruse. Jack fought another fighter named Tom Riley nine days later in Joplin, Missouri. He knocked Riley out cold inside one round. Riley remained unconscious for a nerve-racking ten minutes after the fight.

Dempsey's reputation was now beginning to take hold with sportswriters and the public at large. Kearns' chief goal was to convince enough people that Dempsey should be recognized as the legitimate number one contender for the heavyweight title. Kearns told sportswriters that Dempsey possessed a "killer instinct" and that they should write about it in their columns.

John "the Barber" suddenly slipped out from under a rock and warned Kearns that Dempsey was still under contract with him. Characteristically, Kearns told Reisler to shove off. But Kearns also understood that Reisler needed to be dealt with permanently. He immediately ordered Reisler to provide proof of such a document. Reisler responded by filing a lawsuit against Dempsey and Kearns. He also claimed he had advanced Dempsey five thousand dollars

Dempsey swore that Reisler was lying. Kearns knew Reisler was lying too, but that was not enough to stop Reisler from taking them to court. Desperate to shake off Reisler, Kearns related the whole story to journalist Bill Farnsworth. They both decided that perhaps Colonel Jake Ruppert, co-owner of the New York Yankees baseball team, might be able to help.

The three men met to discuss Dempsey's dilemma. Farnsworth convinced Ruppert that providing the funds needed to make Reisler disappear would be well worth it. Kearns came up with some money and paid Reisler off. He warned him never to threaten Dempsey again with lies and lawsuits.

On May 3, 1918, at the Auditorium in St. Paul Minnesota, Dempsey fought highly respected Billy Miske in a tough battle scheduled for ten rounds. Going into the fight, Jack was not impressed by Miske's appearance as a fighter. Jack figured the fight would not last longer than three rounds. He was shocked, however, to discover just how good a fighter Miske actually was. Miske landed several blows to Dempsey's head which hurt Jack.

"Pull up your socks and smack him down," Kearns screamed at Dempsey between rounds. "Get rid of him. What's the matter with you, anyway? Go out there and take him!"

Dempsey responded to Kearns' urgent warning by becoming much more aggressive. He landed a brutal left hook to Miske's stomach, followed immediately with a swift blow to the head. Miske out boxed Dempsey during most of the fight. Jack tried a maneuver he called the shift, but each time he tried it, Miske stepped out of the way of Jack's attack. The shift refers to a tactic in which a fighter takes a sudden step forward as he drives a blow to the opponent's head or midsection. Dempsey did the best he could, but in the end, the fight was declared a draw after ten rounds. Jack had underestimated Miske's abilities as a boxer before the fight. He swore he would never make that same mistake again.

Dempsey later claimed his poor performance might have been a blessing in disguise. Fred Fulton, who was the number one heavyweight contender, may have been convinced after the fight to take on Jack. He may have figured Dempsey would be easy to beat after his lackadaisical showing against Miske.

On May 22, 1918, Jack faced Dan Ketchell in Excelsior Springs, Colorado. He knocked his victim out inside two rounds. Seven days later he fought a Canadian boxer named Arthur Pelkey at the Stockyards Stadium in Denver, Colorado. He knocked his opponent out inside two minutes of the first round. Pelkey's claim to fame is the fact that at one time he had been hailed as a "Great White Hope." In 1913 in Calgary, Canada, he had killed a well-regarded fighter named Luther McCarthy. Since killing McCarthy, Pelkey's boxing career went into a tailspin. He had been knocked out in ten of his last thirteen bouts prior to meeting Dempsey. This further added fuel to the assertion that

Kearns was deliberately "padding" Dempsey's record.

Boxing was under fire by many progressive groups in the country. These groups claimed that paying to see a fight while America was at war was morally unjustifiable. Kearns responded to these accusations by donating even more money to charitable organizations such as the Red Cross.

Jack filed for divorce because he felt Maxine had essentially deserted him. She was nowhere to be found and Dempsey wanted to legally end their relationship. Maxine accepted the divorce without a fight.

Over the next several weeks Dempsey took on Kid McCarty, Bob Devere, and Dan "Porky" Flynn, another Great White Hope from yesteryear. He destroyed each of them in the first round. Regarding the Flynn fight, Kearns told reporters for the Atlanta newspapers that "You fellows picked up a real tough bird for Dempsey to battle, the toughest in the game."

On the same card as the Dempsey-Flynn fight was a despicable "sporting event" called a Battle Royal. The "event" took place in Atlanta, Georgia. A typical Battle Royal comprised of anywhere between ten to twenty young black men. They would stand together in the ring and battle each other until only one man was left standing. After the event the crowd would throw coins at the winner as a token of their appreciation. One reporter wrote that the nine black youths involved that day "fought like little black demons."

Dempsey's next fight was against a very formable fighter, Fred Fulton, the "Minnesota Plasterer." He was considered the number one heavyweight contender. Fulton hit hard and had an impressive 84-inch reach. Kearns advised Jack to "go in low at his belly and when he jabs down at you, cross him with your right."

Promoting the fight proved to be extremely diffi-cult. It was originally scheduled to be held in Danbury, Connecticut, but the governor refused to allow the fight to be held in his state. After several more attempts to sell the event failed, a little town in New Jersey came to the rescue.

The match was scheduled to take place on July 27, 1918, at the Federal League Ball Park in Harrison, New Jersey. Realizing just how important this fight meant, Jack immediately started training hard at Long Branch, New Jersey. Not wanting to take any chances, Kearns hired the highly regarded Jimmy De Forest as Jack's trainer. De Forest fine-tuned Dempsey's hitting and blocking skills. Kearns also hired two seasoned sparring partners, Jamaica Kid and Jim Johnson. After two months of grueling roadwork on the beach and sparring with top-notch sparring partners, Jack was ready to destroy any man in the ring. He even knocked out the huge, tough sparring partner, Battling Jim Johnson.

Jimmy De Forest played a pivotal role in Jack's devel-opment as a fighter. As Dempsey recalled years later, De Forest's "career went clear back to the days of Peter Jackson and London prize-ring rules. Getting instruction from him was like taking a post-graduate course in boxing. He was a regular little Foxy Grandpa of the ring, with an unlit cigar in the corner of his mouth. He would spend whole days on this or that fine point of hitting or blocking, feint-ing or footwork. We'd take a single blow apart, analyze all the motions that went into it, and try to make changes that would improve it. Then I'd practice the changes we'd decided on, perhaps for a couple of hours, while De Forest watched and commented."

The fight failed to attract the big spenders, so the expensive seats were quickly filled with lower-priced ticket holders. The fight drew a scant ten thousand spectators. Kearns and Dempsey were forced to accept less than the promised $12,500 guarantee from the promoter of the fight. Kearns' share was half of that amount and another portion was allocated toward what he called "expenses." Dempsey knew exactly how he was going to spend his earnings. For quite some time he had planned to buy his mother a new home in Salt Lake City.

On July 21, 1918, just one week before the big fight, Kearns came to Dempsey with bad news. "The fight's off," Kearns advised Jack. "Those people can't get the guarantee up," he explained. Dempsey told Kearns to accept a percentage. He desperately needed the money for the home he wanted to buy his mother. Kearns advised him that perhaps he could get twenty-five percent, which Kearns calculated to be about ten to fifteen thousand dollars. Jack ordered Kearns to accept a percentage of the gate.

Dempsey knew Fulton had a good left hook and could seriously hurt a fighter with his right. He had even beaten the man Dempsey feared most, the great Sam Langford. Although Fred Fulton was taller than Dempsey and had a commanding reach advantage, he suffered from one hugely important defect. He had a glass jaw. The fighter was made to order for Jack.

A riot occurred just before the fight started. There were quite a few high-priced seats still available. Realizing this, many low-priced ticket holders rushed to fill the better seats. Pandemonium broke out and the bout was nearly called off.

Jack spent quite a bit of time warming up before the fight. He firmly believed he might be able to surprise the larger, heavier Fulton who, in Dempsey's view, probably had not warmed up sufficiently before the fight. Dempsey had the look of a wild-eyed crazed killer as he stared intensely at Fulton. Immediately after the bell sounded, Jack rushed across the ring and landed a pulverizing left hook to Fulton's body and followed it up with a deadly right to Fulton's chin. Fulton dropped to the canvas in eighteen seconds of the first round. Referee Johnny Eckhardt counted Fulton out. Dempsey and Kearns were paid nine thousand dollars.

Dempsey was now considered the undisputed top contender for the heavyweight crown. Jess Willard, however, was not impressed with Jack's victory. He told reporters that "I'd like to fight Dempsey…He is not going to win the championship in twenty-three seconds. No, not in one hour and twenty-three seconds."

Immediately after the fight, frenzied fans hailed Jack as their hero. He was staying at the Robert Treat Hotel in Newark at the time. Dempsey experienced his first taste of hero-worship. He later related, "I was almost mobbed. The crowd wanted autographs, pictures, anything. They actually tore my shirt and took pieces of it away as souvenirs. They nearly wrecked the hotel. It was almost a riot."

This period represented a milestone in Dempsey's career. For the rest of his life, boxing fans would admire his exploits in the ring like no other champion before or since. Dempsey's share of the nine thousand dollars came to $5,000. He immediately rushed home to Salt Lake City and bought his mother the home he always wanted her to have. Jack was broke once again, but he was also very happy.

Jess Willard had planned to fight Fred Fulton for the title. Now it appeared Willard would have to fight Dempsey because Jack had catapulted his way to the top of the heavyweight division in fairly short order. Kearns scouted around for a promoter willing to stage the match between his fighter and Jess Willard.

Dempsey desperately wanted to fight Willard for the title. He knew he had a very good shot at beating Willard. The champion, however, played hard to get. In the meantime, Dempsey decided to fight any and all comers. Tough fighters like Terry Kellar, Jack Moran, Gunboat Smith, and Billy Miske all went down in defeat against Dempsey's terrible onslaught.

Kearns arranged for his fighter to face Willie Meehan in the Civic Auditorium in San Francisco. Meehan was in a lot better shape this time around, probably due to his stint in the Navy. Meehan won the decision after four rounds. $18,000 was raised for a Navy relief fund. Dempsey was unfazed by the loss because of his astounding performances in his most recent battles against top contenders for the heavyweight title.

The very next day Dempsey faced Jack Moran at the Moana Springs Arena in Reno, Nevada. Dempsey promptly knocked out Jack Moran in one round. Kearns put a temporary halt on Jack's strenuous training sessions because he feared he might grow stale. Jack happily took several weeks off from training. But his idleness did not last long. Kearns arranged for Jack to face Battling Levinsky, the light heavyweight champion of the world. The fight was slated to take place on November 6, 1918, at the Olympia Athletic Club in Philadelphia, Pennsylvania.

Cody Drennen, a representative of the Sun Shipyard in Philadelphia, and a U.S. government representative, asked Kearns for his permission to allow Jack to pose for a recruitment poster. Kearns wholeheartedly agreed. The next day Jack was provided with striped overalls to wear over his clothes. Several photographs were taken.

The next day, Jack was shocked to see his image in the newspapers. The picture showed Jack posing in a shipyard work uniform. Clearly displayed in the photograph, however, were Jack's very shiny patent leather shoes. Dempsey rightfully feared an enormous backlash against what he had been trying to represent in his recruiting effort. He feared his draft deferment would come back to haunt him. Kearns advised Jack not to worry about any possible fallout.

Battling Levinsky had the distinction of having never been knocked out in his entire career. He was also the light heavyweight champion of the world. The fight was scheduled for six rounds, the absolute limit a fight could go in the state of Pennsylvania. In the first round, Jack noticed Levinsky was not able to evade many of his punches. Levinsky was successful in landing left jabs to Dempsey's face, but by and large the blows were ineffective. Just before the first round ended, Dempsey unleashed a barrage of blows that staggered Levinsky.

In the second round, Jack landed hard rights and lefts to Levinsky's head and body. The blows weakened Levinsky's resolve to survive, let alone win. Near the end of the round, Dempsey let loose with a hard blow to his opponent's stomach. Levinsky immediately dropped to the canvas in excruciating pain. It was the first time Levinsky had ever been knocked down in the ring. Miraculously,

Levinsky survived the round. In the third round, Dempsey landed a hard left to Levinsky's head and down he went. The referee stopped the fight and Jack was declared the winner by a knockout.

On November 18, 1918, Jack faced Porky Dan Flynn at the Olympia Athletic Club in Philadelphia. He effortlessly knocked Flynn out in the first round. Jack had apparently become an expert at catching fighters cold with his unexpected, explosive attack.

Dempsey faced Billy Miske again on November 28, 1918, at the Olympia Athletic Club in Philadelphia. The bout was scheduled for six rounds in accordance with state law. Although Dempsey was the aggressor throughout the fight, Miske was able to hang on long enough to barely survive the pounding he received from Jack. Miske basically clinched his way out of an almost certain knockout. The official ruling for the fight was a no decision. Sportswriters, however, ruled overwhelmingly in Dempsey's favor.

Over the next several weeks, Dempsey fought non-contenders in some exhibition bouts. He also faced Carl Morris, a man Dempsey absolutely detested. The fight took place on December 16, 1918, at the Louisiana Auditorium in New Orleans. Just after the bell sounded, Morris rushed toward Dempsey, pushing him into the ropes. Morris landed several blows to Dempsey's ribs. The punches hurt Jack and he knew from that moment on Morris was out for blood. Dempsey immediately clinched and when the two fighters separated, Morris rushed Jack again. Morris' stomach was unprotected for just an instant and Dempsey drove a hard left into Morris' solar plexus. Morris dropped to the canvas like a bag of hammers. He desperately tried to get back on his feet but his legs were essentially paralyzed. Referee Remy Dorr counted Morris out. The fight had lasted a mere fourteen seconds of the first round.

On December 30, 1918, Dempsey destroyed Gunboat Smith at the Broadway Auditorium in Buffalo, New York. Dempsey finished him off with a quick knockout in the second round. By now Jack had developed a philosophy that would last him for the rest of his boxing career. The best defense is a good offence. He knew that at any moment in a fight he could get tagged with a lucky punch. In order to lessen that eventuality, he would try to take out the other fellow early.

CHAPTER FOUR

TOLEDO, OHIO, 1919

*Challenger Jack Dempsey viciously attacks champion
Jess Willard and goes on to win the heavyweight title fight.*

Throughout the early months of 1919, Dempsey took on five opponents, knocking each of them out in the first round. It was becoming obvious to everyone that Jess Willard had to face Dempsey in the ring sooner than later. Even Willard understood that Jack Dempsey had now become the number one heavyweight contender. Willard could no longer escape the harsh ridicule being heaped on him by the sportswriters and public at large.

Kearns and Dempsey began making promotional rounds in big cities instead of smaller towns. Kearns wanted to reach as many people per event as possible during their publicity tour. Beginning in 1919, Kearns tried another mode of publicity, the vaudeville circuit. They joined Barney Gerard's American Burlesques. Kearns typically came out on stage and explained to the audience why every youngster in America should take up boxing as a sport. After he finished his spiel he would introduce Jack as the next heavyweight champion. Then Dempsey came out on stage, waved to the crowd and proceeded to jump rope, hammer away at some heavy bags, and shadow box. After Jack displayed his boxing prowess, Kearns stepped forward and challenged anyone in the audience to box three rounds with Dempsey. If the challenger lasted three rounds, he would receive one thousand dollars.

One night a man named Curley challenged Dempsey. He was huge but Dempsey didn't appear to be concerned. Jack allowed the man to last one round. He threw a vicious left hook at Curley's stomach and down he went. The challenger grabbed the stage curtain as he crashed to the floor. The ring and the stage scenery collapsed all around him.

The audience ate it up.

In the meantime, Tex Rickard carefully searched for a legitimate contender for the heavyweight title. Rickard was determined not to promote a title fight involving a black contender. Sam McVey, Bill Tate, and Harry Wills were among the very best black fighters from that era. There were very few fighters worth considering from among white heavyweights. Gunboat Smith was way past his prime as was Carl Morris, Willie Meehan, Billy Miske, and Terry Kellar.

Through the process of elimination, Tex Rickard observed that Jack Dempsey had the best recent record of all white heavyweight contenders. Rickard, however, was seriously concerned about Jack's small stature as compared to Jess Willard's. "Every time I see you," he said to Jack, "you look smaller to me." It was probably not meant to be a put-down but rather a serious concern he had about Dempsey's ability to take on the behemoth Willard.

Tex Rickard couldn't seem to shake his reservations about Dempsey's chances of surviving in the ring against Jess Willard. Dempsey may have had youth and talent on his side, but Jess Willard was much bigger and stronger than Jack. Perhaps more importantly, Willard had killed an opponent six years earlier. Jess had thrown a vicious right-hand uppercut that nearly took the head off of his opponent, John "Bull" Young. Young died the next day, ostensibly from a brain hemorrhage. Willard was immediately arrested and charged with manslaughter. The charges against big Jess were subsequently dropped.

Sensing the vaudeville circuit was not the best way to publicize Dempsey, Kearns decided to go to New York "to see who or what I can hustle up." Kearns returned two days later with promising news. He informed Jack that Tex Rickard was now convinced that a fight between Dempsey and Willard would draw a huge crowd. He managed to assure Rickard that he would make an enormous amount of money from the fight. Rickard raised again his concern that Dempsey was too small to go up against Willard. He might even get killed in the ring and that would be very bad for boxing. Kearns pointed out that the champion hadn't fought anyone for quite some time and that he was out of shape. Rickard finally bought into Kearns' argument.

Tex Rickard firmly believed, after a great deal of persuasion from Kearns, that he could draw a huge crowd to a Willard-Dempsey bout. He reasoned that Willard was so hated and despised for not fighting, people would gladly show up at a title fight just to boo him. Moreover, Rickard was prepared to offer the champion a great deal of money for a second defense of the heavyweight title.

Rickard's wife wrote a book about her husband called *Everything Happened to Him*. In that book, Mrs. Rickard related comments Tex Rickard had made to her regarding the significance of a Willard-Dempsey fight and why he thought it would be a huge draw.

"Haven't you learned yet that I know how to pick winners? If I could get someone in the ring with Willard that would really fight, I'd pack in more people than ever saw a prize fight in history outside of them Roman things you was tellin' me about. I tell you, the people in this country are still all tied up in knots inside on account of the war. They want a chance to holler and get excited. I've studied this over a long time."

Jack was excited to hear about the opportunity of finally facing Willard. His excitement subsided drastically, however, when Kearns confessed that he had told Rickard his fighter would be willing to fight for nothing. Jack couldn't believe Kearns would stoop to this level of desperation. This incident would turn out to be one of many instances in which Kearns and Dempsey vehemently disagreed about money.

Kearns and Dempsey were appearing at the Arch Street Theater in Philadelphia when word arrived from Tex. Rickard wanted them to meet him immediately in New York to discuss terms. Rickard offered Kearns a guarantee of $25,000 for the proposed fight between Willard and Dempsey. Kearns laughed at the figure and told him it was much too low. Kearns wanted $50,000. Rickard thought Kearns' figure was ridiculously too high. Rickard explained that the larger the purse, the greater the gamble. The fight might not draw enough fans to justify a large purse.

"Besides," Rickard reminded Kearns, "you and I know you could afford to fight for nothing. If Jack here can beat him, it'll be worth half a million to you fellows inside a year."

Kearns suggested that the sportswriters should decide whether or not a Willard-Dempsey fight made any sense. Rickard agreed with Kearns' proposal. Tex was still very concerned that Jack was much too small to fight the giant Jess Willard. He seriously thought Jack might get killed in the ring.

Kearns called for a press conference the following day. Many highly respected news writers assembled to hear what Rickard and Kearns had to discuss. Included in the press conference were Gene Fowler, Rube Goldberg, and Damon Runyon, Jack's old friend. Rickard began the meeting by declaring that Jess Willard had decided to fight Jack Dempsey for the title and that Willard would receive $100,000. He claimed that promoting such a fight was a huge gamble for him. To help compensate for that risk, he suggested Dempsey should fight Willard for nothing. Kearns seethed in disbelief at Rickard's audacity. He found it very difficult to contain himself.

Rickard, not wanting to seem too conniving, suggested that perhaps Dempsey and company should receive $10,000 or even $15,000 for the fight. Kearns immediately fired back at Rickard. He reminded him that it was he, Jack Kearns, who ultimately persuaded Rickard to speak with Willard about the possibility of fighting Dempsey. He went on to explain that Jack had recently knocked out several top-notch heavyweight contenders. He reminded everyone that Willard had not fought anyone for several years. Instead, he had decided to tour with Buffalo Bill's Wild West Show. Kearns suggested that because of these reasons, Jack deserved to be paid "at least half as much as Willard."

The sportswriters huddled together to discuss what they had just heard. Occasionally someone in the group looked up and glanced at Dempsey, perhaps trying to decide if he looked tough enough to fight the champion. Finally, Rickard offered the challenger $25,000. There was no room for negotiation. Kearns quickly responded by asking for $30,000. Fair is fair he claimed. Kearns warned Rickard not to be a cheap scoundrel. The final decision was left up to the sportswriters. They agreed that $27,500 was reasonable. Dempsey was elated. This was perhaps more money than he had earned in his entire career.

Rickard was not pleased with the outcome. He was responsible for owing both fighters a total of $127,500. He was unsure how he could come up with such a large sum of money. Not only did he need to promote the fight, he also had to find a venue for the championship bout. He was deeply worried.

Kearns advised Rickard that he would try to help him raise cash for the proposed match. Kearns contacted everyone he knew who might be interested in supporting the fight. Unfortunately, New York was not a viable option because the state had very strict legislative rules regarding boxing. Addison Q. Thatcher, a prominent member of the Toledo Athletic Club, told Kearns that Toledo, Ohio would be the perfect setting for such an event. Governor James Cox, however, would have the final say in such a matter.

According to Kearns, many people were mistakenly in awe of Willard's size. The fact that the champion stood half a foot taller than Jack and weighed at least seventy pounds more didn't matter. They had many detractors, however. Bat Masterson chimed in, stating that he thought true heavyweight champions should be bulky. Kearns argued that although Willard was powerfully built, it was questionable as to whether he could defend himself against someone as agile, hungry, and ferocious as a young Jack Dempsey.

Rickard and Kearns cornered Cox at an Elks convention in Ohio. They managed to persuade the governor that the fight would be extremely beneficial for Toledo's businesses. Moreover, the publicity would put Toledo on the map. Subsequently, Kearns received $100,000 from Frank Flournoy, an associate of Thatcher's.

Rickard held a press conference in New York. He

proclaimed that the Willard-Dempsey fight would take place in Toledo, Ohio. Immediately after the announcement, the Ohio Ministerial Association denounced the fight as immoral. Concerned that bad publicity might derail the bout, Rickard swung into action. He asked Major A.J.D. Biddle, an important and influential proponent of boxing to see if he could persuade the organization to stop its crusade against the fight. Biddle succeeded, but he wanted some favors from Tex. Rickard agreed that Ollie Pecord would be the referee and W. Warren Barbour, a future U.S. senator, would assume the role of timekeeper.

Tex Rickard was hopeful that the Willard-Dempsey fight would become the first million-dollar gate in boxing history. Rickard hired James McLaughlin to construct a wooden stadium that could hold 80,000 customers. McLaughlin had experience building similar arenas in Reno and San Francisco. The arena in Toledo included a makeshift hospital and a protected section designed specifically for females. Unfortunately, he made the mistake of using new lumber. Consequently, the rise in temperature on the day of the fight allowed sap to ooze from the lumber.

Dempsey trained at the Overland Club under the direction of Jimmy De Forest. De Forest was careful not to over train Jack because he might grow stale. He made Jack work out every other week. Jack was free to do almost anything he wanted in between the weeks he trained. Typically, he told stories to children or played baseball on the beach.

Dempsey was getting a lot of good play in the press. One reporter wrote that "there has seldom been a fight where opinion is so divided for both fighters, though Dempsey's friends seem to be in the majority. It is doubtful if there has ever been a heavyweight fighter who could move as fast as Dempsey. He moves like a featherweight. But Willard sentiment is growing, for Willard has been so positive he is in good shape that even the most skeptical are beginning to believe him."

Kearns began publicly needling Willard. He ridiculed him to the point where Willard had to respond. Big Jess criticized Jack's so called ability to knock out his opponents seconds into the first round.

"What good fighter gets knocked out in the first round?" he mused. "I hope he comes rushing at me. I'll fix him good."

Willard finally arrived in Toledo to train for the title fight. Curiously, he didn't have a manager with him. This may have been due to either Willard's overconfidence, frugality, or both. The champ had the reputation of hating people. He stayed to himself when he wasn't training.

Dempsey trained hard for the fight. He rose early and jogged seven or more miles each morning before breakfast. His meals consisted mainly of meat and vegetables. He took a short nap after each meal and then jogged several more miles. He was amazed at the number of people who watched him run. Fans paid to watch Dempsey work out and spar with Jamaica Kid and Big Bill Tate. Drugs, booze, and women were forbidden in Dempsey's training camp. In the evening, everyone settled in and talked about the upcoming fight while others played a friendly game of gin rummy.

Willard invited Dempsey to watch him train. Kearns thought that was a particularly bad idea. He thought perhaps Jack might become adversely affected by the champion's size and strength. Kearns received word that Willard was not training as hard as Dempsey. Encouraged that Willard might not be able to withstand Dempsey's punishing assaults, Kearns bet $10,000 that Jack would knock out the champ in the first round. The bet was hard to turn down because the odds were 10 to 1 against that eventuality.

To kill time, Max Kaplan, Jimmy De Forest, and Jack occasionally sang and danced. Kearns passed the time drinking and talking non-stop to anyone willing to listen. Kearns became a nervous wreck whenever Jack took a spin in his Stutz. Another time Jamaica Kid opened a cut over Jack's right eye while sparring. Dempsey reassured a panicked Kearns that he would be fine.

Jack was advised to wear headgear in order to lessen the chance of a serious head injury. Kearns thought the idea was ridiculous. Dempsey thought otherwise because he knew the equipment protected his brows and ears. Willard enjoyed joking about Dempsey's headgear and belittled the challenger every time the subject came up.

Dempsey turned twenty-four on June 24 and everyone in the camp celebrated his birthday. Kearns referred to Jack's physical condition as being "hard as a keg of nails." He observed that the champion's midsection looked "a shade soft." Although Willard was a monster of a man, Kearns believed Dempsey was quicker and harder to hit than Willard. Amazingly, Jack's father thought his own son would lose to Willard. Hyrum's opinion about his son's chances in the ring disturbed Jack.

Jack woke up early the morning of the fight. He trained harder than at any time in his career. Kearns advised Dempsey not to show any sign of anxiety because the newspaper boys might try to sensationalize it. Kearns was pleased to see that his fighter was "as brown as his Indian forebears, quick and impatient of movement, and his usual stoic self. He had been trained to just the right edge."

"How's it, Champ?" Kearns asked Jack.

"All right," Dempsey replied. "Just fine."

"Good," Kearns told his fighter. "Just take it easy and conserve your energy."

During the weigh-in Dempsey was careful not to look up at Willard. He looked down at his feet. Jack's official weight was 187 pounds. Willard weighed in at an astounding 245 pounds. Willard was a good five inches taller than Jack. Dempsey later indicated that before the weigh-in, he gorged himself with bananas and hid rocks in his boxing trunks in order to appear heavier. He claimed his actual weight was only 180 pounds.

Willard looked down at his victim with complete and utter distain. The next time the two would meet would be at 4 p.m. Willard was a 5 to 4 favorite. He was certain he would annihilate the challenger. He even had the audacity to ask Kearns for legal immunity in case he killed Dempsey in the ring.

On July 4, 1919, the day of the championship fight, the temperature rose to an unbearable 106 degrees. Not surprisingly, vendors sold out of their beverages and ice cream in less than an hour. Tex Rickard bragged about his brand-new arena. He claimed that if each board was placed so that the ends touched lengthwise, the distance would be the same as the distance from Chicago to New York.

Thousands of boxing fans watched preliminary bouts that began every thirty minutes in the sweltering heat. A brass band was hired to play between bouts but the instruments were too hot to touch. A U.S. Army Balloon Corps blimp floated high above the ring. A dare devil Army aviator performed death-defying stunts while in mid-air.

Tickets sold for as high as 60 dollars and as low as 2 dollars. There was even a special section in the stadium reserved exclusively for women. Bat Masterson, one of the legends of the Old West, was on hand. He had the privilege of collecting customer's guns and knives. Assisting him was none other than Wyatt Earp, the legendary lawman of the West. Several angry customers put up a fight when they were asked to surrender their weapons.

Dempsey later explained exactly how he was going to fight Willard. "I would hold my low crouch," he related. "Cowboy Jess would expect me to come at him with a rush as I had attacked so many opponents. Well, I wouldn't do it. I would be cautious. The change in tactics might disconcert him. I wanted him to attack. I wanted him coming toward me, fast, with all his great bulk and momentum, so that my own punches would carry that much more sting. I would try to force him to lead. As opportunity offered I would charge in to close quarters and try to sink a staggering punch to the solar plexus. If I succeeded in landing a blow hard enough to double him up, I could then hit for the head. I would have to be quick in order to get in and out before he could clinch and tire me with his great weight in that heat. I would also have to avoid being knocked out myself by having a punch from his powerful arms land where it could turn the trick."

Jimmy De Forest taped Dempsey's hands while two of Willard's men witnessed the procedure. One of Willard's witnesses was a huge man named Walter Monaghan. He watched carefully as Jack's hands were taped with gauze and adhesive tape. Not wanting to take anything for granted, Monaghan followed Dempsey all the way to his corner in the ring. Likewise, people from Jack's camp watched as Willards's hands were taped. Kearns waved at Willard and the champion looked at him in disgust.

"Let's get on with it," Willard bellowed. He was very unimpressed with Kearns' attempt at cordiality. Kearns noticed that Willard's handlers appeared inexperienced as they nervously taped Willard's huge hands. Kearns offered to help wrap the champ's hands with bandages, but Willard waved him away.

"Get away from me," Willard sneered.

Kearns simply smiled, pleased that his needling had bothered Jess. But Kearns was not through with his sarcasm. He advised Willard's handlers to cool the champion's hands with a wet sponge. Willard had reached his boiling point.

"Why don't you get the hell out of here?" Willard yelled.

"Just trying to help," Kearns replied as he shrugged. "But I got a right in here and I'll stay til the job's finished."

Kearns was still seething over the remark Willard had made to him about not wanting to be responsible for killing Dempsey in the ring. "He couldn't kill a midget if they gave him an axe," Kearns told the newspaper reporters. "Why, I'd fight the bum myself, and for nothing, but I might cripple him. It's that big tub of lard who's gonna be slaughtered."

It was now fight time. The crowd cheered as Jack jogged down the aisle leading to the ring. Men wore straw hats and white short-sleeved shirts. Many of the female fans held umbrellas to shield themselves from the blistering sun. Kearns looked out into the crowd and saw a sea of straw skimmers and an occasional derby.

Jack stood nervously in his corner, waiting for the champion to make his grand entrance. The sun beat down on the crowd of excited and curious fight fans. Dempsey gratefully stood under a huge beach umbrella which bore advertisements Kearns cleverly had sold to merchants for $25 a foot. The challenger looked like a caged lion, ready to tear into his prey. He appeared a lot lighter than the 187 pounds he was supposed to have weighed. Dempsey scowled as he looked out into the crowd. He resented the fact that Willard had kept him waiting for so long. Kearns advised Jack to take it easy.

"Relax, Champ," Kearns warned Dempsey. "The fat bum is probably scared to come out." Trying to steady his nerves, the challenger stood very still and stared down at his feet in order to focus his attention away from the task at hand. Deep in his heart he knew he had a shot at winning the heavyweight title, but he feared that Willard might hammer home a blow that could end the fight at any moment. The challenger feared the unexpected as many abhor the encroachment of death.

Dempsey recalled after the fight that "I thought I was going to be sick to my stomach. Willard's back was a solid wall. His fists look like they were twice as high in the air as I was tall. I saw the muscles standing out on his back. Fat? He was in terrific shape. I said to myself, 'This guy is liable to kill me. I'm twenty-four years old and I might get killed.'"

Jack was truly amazed at Willard's size and stature. According to Dempsey, the champion appeared to be in fantastic shape. "He was gigantic," Jack recalled, "but proportioned like an Apollo. Tremendous shoulders, arms, legs, and torso outlined in muscle. Skin tanned almost as brown as my own. Not an ounce of fat. Suddenly all the stories that had come to me of his inadequate training seemed no more than reports to bolster my courage."

The champion had a sure-fire plan to handily defeat his victim. He realized Jack liked to rush his opponent immediately after the bell sounded in an attempt to score a quick knock out. He knew Jack enjoyed catching his opponent cold early in the fight because he didn't like to take chances with anyone. Even a sub-par heavyweight had a reasonable chance of knocking Jack out with a lucky punch.

"He'll come tearing at me, but I'm seventy or eighty pounds heavier than the boy. I'll have my left out. He'll have to watch out for my left when he's tearing in. Then I'll hit him with a right uppercut. That will be the end," Jess proudly boasted.

The crowd shouted hysterically as the champion entered the ring. Many ringsiders claimed that Willard looked rather bored. He had kept a very nervous and pent up Dempsey waiting for so very long. He dropped his robe, turned away from the challenger, and raised his huge arms into the air while fans cheered. Dempsey felt sick as he watched this mountain of a man tower over his entourage. He remembered that "everything outside the ropes of the ring disappeared. I was actually going to fight for the heavyweight championship of the world!"

The fighters were ordered to approach the middle of the ring for instructions. Willard towered over the much smaller Dempsey. It must have appeared to many in the audience that Jack was totally out of his league. He was being led to the slaughter. Dempsey appeared unfazed by Willard's huge frame. Jack stared at Willard's belly during the ring instructions. His mind seemed elsewhere. He couldn't have cared less about the ring instructions.

The referee, Ollie Pecord, explained to both combatants the basic rules of engagement in the ring. "Keep your punches up," he warned. "Break clean from the clinches. Good luck to you both." Dempsey refused to look up at the giant Willard. He may have speculated that he had underestimated Willard's chances of winning the fight.

W. Warren Barbour sounded the bell to begin the first round and started keeping time with his stopwatch. The fighters didn't hear the bell because a rope had been inadvertently sandwiched in between the ring-bell clapper and the bell. Apparently, this was the work of a sloppy workman who had been charged with stretching new canvas over the ring's flooring. In a panic, Barbour blew on a drill sergeant's whistle. He yelled up at a very confused Jess Willard, "Go ahead! Go ahead!"

Barbour, still upset over the mishap, forgot to reset his stopwatch. Willard kept looking over his left shoulder, confused as to what had happened. After what seemed like an eternity, the bell rang a second time and both fighters left their corners to do battle.

Round one began with both fighters feeling each other out. Willard threw a right at Dempsey's head, perhaps trying to end the fight right then and there. Jack quickly backed away from Jess and continued to circle the champion. Dempsey surprised Willard by not rushing him as was expected. Instead, Dempsey showed off his boxing skills by fighting out of a crouch, constantly bobbing and weaving, quickly moving in and out of harm's way. Then Willard and Dempsey got down to business and began exchanging punches. Jess had an exceedingly difficult time setting himself up so that he could land a haymaker to Dempsey's jaw. Neither fighter appeared to be hurt by the other's attacks.

Dempsey suddenly exploded with a hard right, a hard left, another hard right to Willard's midsection, followed by a hard left to Willard's jaw. The champ dropped to the canvas from the unexpected barrage of blows. Shocked spectators quickly rose to their feet, screaming and waving their arms hysterically. No one had ever witnessed such savagery in the ring. Willard looked utterly stunned and confused as the referee counted over him. Popular sportswriter, Grantland Rice, wrote that the champion "wore a dazed and foolish look, a simple half-smile crowning a mouth that was twitching in pain and bewilderment."

Jess slowly rose to his feet, wounded but still in the fight. His cheekbone had been severely shattered in several places and his face was beginning to look ghastly. Smelling blood, the challenger rushed the champion again with a barrage of fists and fury. With Willard's back against the ropes, Dempsey landed lefts and rights at Willard's face, seemingly at will. The champion appeared totally helpless. He had absolutely no defense against this kind of hellish brutality. Willard dropped to the canvas a second time. Teeth sprayed from the champion's swollen mouth. One hysterical fan reportedly screamed, "Give me one of the big guy's teeth. I want his teeth!"

Willard rose slowly and cautiously as Dempsey prepared for another brutal assault. Once again Dempsey hammered away at Willard's body and the champion dropped to the canvas a third time. Willard's face was now a bloody pulp, his blood dripping onto the canvas. Dempsey triumphantly stood over Willard as the champion tried to crawl away from him. Just as Willard lifted both knees off the canvas, Dempsey landed more blows to Willard's head and down he went for a fourth time.

Dempsey was forbidden to punch Willard while he was down, but that didn't stop him from hammering away at him as he rose to his feet. The neutral-corner rule was non-existent. Somehow the big guy managed to pull himself up by grabbing onto the ropes. Several onlookers who had witnessed enough carnage screamed "Stop it! Stop it!"

Dempsey rushed at the wounded Willard and smashed him up against the ropes. He unleashed a fresh barrage of hard rights and lefts to the champion's ghastly battered face. More screams of "Stop it!" erupted from the crowd. They had never seen such utter savagery in the ring. The champion fell a fifth time to the blood-soaked canvas.

The instant Willard rose to his feet, Dempsey unleashed more unholy hell on Jess. Desperately attempting to avoid more punishment, Willard staggered over to another corner. As he did so, Dempsey threw hard, overhead rights to Willard's head. Jess hit the deck a sixth time. As Willard grabbed the ropes in an attempt to pull himself up, Dempsey unleashed a fresh barrage of blows at his victim. The champion dropped to the canvas a seventh time. He sat completely helpless in the corner, spitting blood, apparently unable or unwilling to rise. The referee started counting over the disfigured champion. When Pecord reached the count of ten, the fight appeared to be over. The crowd screamed hysterically as the referee raised Jack's fist in triumph. The knockout would go down as the quickest in the history of heavyweight title fights.

Kearns and the rest of Jack's team threw their arms around Dempsey as they congratulated him on his stunning victory. Kearns screamed at his fighter, "Jack, you're the champ!" Dempsey rushed out of the ring to avoid being crushed by over-zealous fans. Amazingly, the fight was not over. The bell had actually been rung before Willard was counted out but no one in the ring had heard it. Apparently, the bell sounded just as Pecord's count reached seven.

Dempsey, tired but victorious, stumbled on his way out of the ring and into the aisle leading up to his dressing room. He suddenly heard Kearns screaming at him to come back. Jack turned around and saw Kearns frantically waving his arms at Dempsey to return to the ring.

"It's still on!" Kearns screamed. Dempsey tried to make sense of it all. He had just destroyed Willard and now Kearns wanted him back in the ring. Jack thought that perhaps he wanted him to box some more so that it wouldn't appear the fight was fake. After all, it was very unusual for a heavyweight champion, especially one as huge as Willard, to be beaten into submission by a much smaller opponent in the first round. Kearns frantically explained to Dempsey that no one had heard the bell go off ending the first round.

"The bell saved him," Kearns explained. "The round ended at the count of eight."

This was bad news for Dempsey. He was arm weary from all the punches thrown at Willard. Had he not been in the ring by the start of the second round, Jack would have been disqualified. If that had happened, Willard would

have kept his title and may have refused to face Dempsey
again anytime soon.

The bell sounded for the second round and Dempsey
moved toward Willard very deliberately. He was exhausted
from his tremendous effort in the last round. Dempsey
continued hammering away at Willard's head and torso.
Willard hit Jack with a solid right-hand uppercut that hurt
Jack. Dempsey recovered quickly and attacked Willard like
a hungry panther. The champion was a bloody mess. His
entire face was red and swollen and much of his body was
covered with unsightly welts. Dempsey landed a hard left
to Willard's eye, causing it to close. Willard miraculously
survived the second round.

Surprisingly, Jess answered the bell for the third
round. Dempsey continued his onslaught. "When the bell
sounded for the third round," Dempsey recounted years
later in a book he had written, "my arms felt like lead
weights. Willard was now an object of pity, completely at
my mercy. He was spent and he had made no attempt to
fight back. I pounded rights and lefts to the head and the
body while he tried unsuccessfully to cover up. He threw a
left uppercut, but it was too late. The weaker he looked, the
stronger I felt. I knew it was almost over. I hit him again
and he staggered, about to go down, when he was saved by
the bell. I went back to my corner on legs that felt like rubber. I looked over toward Willard. His face was distorted
by a broken cheekbone and he was having trouble holding
his head up. I felt sick. I hadn't realized that my inner fury
could do so much damage." ·

Willard didn't answer the bell for the fourth round.
Ike O'Neal and Walter Monaghan had decided their fighter

had been punished beyond recognition and threw in a bloody towel to officially end the slaughter.

Jack Dempsey had now become the new heavyweight champion. The crowd roared their approval. Several spectators cruelly shouted "Quitter" at Jess. Dempsey knew otherwise. He had never seen a fighter take as much punishment in the ring as had Willard. Amazingly, Jack was completely unmarked. He was lifted onto several fans' shoulders and carried straight to his dressing room. Jack was pushed and shoved by well-wishers trying to shake his hand or slap him on the back.

"The right side of Willard's face was a pulp," wrote Damon Runyon after the horrendous beating Willard received. "The right eye of the fallen champion was completely hidden behind that bloody smear. His left eye peered over a lump of flesh in grotesque fashion. The great body of the giant was splotched with red patches. They were the aftermath of Dempsey's gloves thumping there and giving back a hollow sound as they thumped. At the feet of the Gargantuan pugilist was a dark spot which was slowly widening on the brown canvas as it was replenished by the drip-drip-drip of blood from the man's wounds. He was flecked with blood from head to toe."

After the bout, Willard graciously congratulated Jack on winning the title. "I was fairly beaten and thoroughly beaten," Willard later commented. "Will I try to recover the championship? I will not because I could not. Dempsey is a great fighter. I know that now. I congratulate him and I wish him luck. My plans? They won't interest people anymore. I'm no longer champion. Now I'm just an ordinary guy."

Dempsey stayed at the Secor Hotel that evening. He barely managed to shower and dress. He was thoroughly exhausted. Jack went to sleep around ten o'clock. He experienced a nightmare that caused him to fall out of bed. He dreamt Willard had knocked him out cold. He turned on the lights and stared at himself in the mirror. His face was not marked up as he had feared.

Dempsey threw some clothes on and ran outside of the hotel. He stood at the corner of Jefferson Street and Lafayette where he spotted a newsboy. Jack noticed the boy had a stack of the latest edition of the *Toledo Blade*. Dempsey anxiously asked the youngster who had won the title fight.

"Aren't you Jack Dempsey?" the boy asked.

Jack informed the boy that he was. Amazed, the boy replied, "You damn, fool! You did!"

Jack gratefully rewarded the newsboy with a dollar and then rushed back to bed. Jack slept soundly the rest of the night.

Willard later told several members of the press that Dempsey must have had something hard in his gloves in order to have inflicted that much damage. Kearns responded to Willard's claims by stating that he was a sore loser. Many years after Kearns and Dempsey split, Kearns made the unsubstantiated claim that Jack's fists were indeed coated with plaster, a claim that would never be proven. For now, at least, Jack "Doc" Kearns was firmly in Jack's corner.

"In his own way," Grantland Rice wrote, "Willard, too, was unbelievable. From ringside it looked as if every one of Dempsey's terrific punches would tear away his head. But for six minutes he stood up and took upon his unprotected jaw an almost countless flurry of punches from a man who is the hardest hitter fighting has ever known."

W.O. McGeehan wrote: "Willard directed his own battle. He had perfect confidence in his bulk and in his strength. There may be those who will argue that he was not properly conditioned. That is utter rot. No man not in the best of condition could have taken that punishment and survived. Only because he went into the ring in perfect shape is Jess Willard alive."

Damon Runyon astutely observed that "a bleeding, trembling, helpless hulk, Jess Willard, the Kansas Giant, this afternoon relinquished his title of heavyweight champion of the world. The end came just as the bell was about to toss him into the fourth round of a mangling at the paws of Jack Dempsey, the young mountain lion in human form, from the Sangre de Cristo Hills of Colorado."

CHAPTER FIVE

FIGHT OF THE CENTURY

French challenger Georges Carpentier shakes hands with champion Jack Dempsey prior to the "Fight of the Century".

Champions and ex-champions heaped praise on the new heavyweight king. Benny Leonard, the lightweight champion at the time, announced that Dempsey "should be champion for some time to come." The magnificent James J. Corbett called Dempsey the "greatest heavyweight since Jim Jeffries was in his prime."

Many gamblers who had bet on the fight fumed afterwards. Tom Jones, Willard's former manager, bet $4,000 on the champion. He recognized Willard's flaws, but was under the impression that he was unbeatable judging by the top contenders. After all, Jess was the man who had put away the great Jack Johnson. Bat Masterson was another sceptic who underestimated Dempsey's abilities. He lost an enormous amount of money on the fight. Upset by his financial woes, he predicted that Dempsey would lose the title in less than a year.

After the fight, Dempsey proclaimed to the world that he would not defend the heavyweight title against any "Negro challenger." Unfortunately, this sentiment was accepted by many boxing fans in America. Dempsey felt certain he could do well in the ring against any fighter, regardless of ethnicity. His statement revealed just how unjust black athletes were treated in the early part of the twentieth century. The lame excuse most white fight managers and promoters used was revealing. Apparently, they didn't want another Jack Johnson in control of the heavyweight title. According to them, the experience had been all too humiliating.

All was not well with Dempsey, however. Grantland Rice, a highly popular writer for the *New York Tribune*, lashed out at Jack. He accused Dempsey of being a slacker during the war. He printed the following in part:

"If he had been a fighting man he would have been in khaki when at twenty-two he had no other responsibilities except to protect his own hide. So let us have no illusions about our new heavyweight champion. He is a marvel in the ring, the greatest boxing or the greatest hitting machine even the old timers have ever seen."

"But he isn't the world's champion fighter. Not by a margin of 50,000 men who either stood or were even ready to stand the test of cold steel and exploding shell for anything from six cents to a dollar a day."

Dempsey was terribly hurt by Rice's attack. He assumed the columnist was unaware of his philanthropy during the war. Jack had made huge donations to the Red Cross and Navy Relief. According to Dempsey, Rice was probably ignorant of the fact that he helped financially support his parents and his wife with what meager savings he could spare. Kearns told Dempsey not to pay heed to Rice's opinions. Kearns would settle scores with Rice himself.

Jack tried to forget Rice's comments as best he could. He focused more on the thousands of telegrams from fans that literally flooded his training camp. Offers from all corners came pouring in as well. Kearns and Dempsey accepted an offer to tour with the reputable Sells-Floto Circus. The movie industry pleaded with Jack to star in their films.

Dempsey was in for some more bad tidings. Kearns informed the champion that they were still broke. "I don't get it," Jack told Kearns. Kearns explained to him that the $27,500 they received from Tex Rickard was all gone.

"While you were training, I needed movement

money," Kearns argued. "Money to move around. Keep the sportswriters on your side. It's important, Champ, to keep the sportswriters on your side." Dempsey wasn't buying any of Kearns' assertions about where his share went.

"Are you telling me you blew the whole twenty-seven five on Runyon and Lardner and the other guys?"

Kearns tried to convince Jack that the payments were necessary. "Champ, when I got you this fight, we didn't have no money of our own. I had to borrow all our movement money from Rickard. That come to eighty-five hundred. Rickard held on to that and give us the rest, nineteen thousand. But then I had to cover the ten thousand dollars we lost on the bet because you couldn't knock out the big bum in the first round."

Dempsey became furious at this point. "I never told you I could knock him out in one round," Dempsey shouted at Kearns. "The guy was never knocked out before by anyone. It was you who said he was a bum, not me. And he ain't a bum. No bum has guts like that guy."

Kearns had an answer for anything Dempsey threw at him. "Anyways, Champ, that bet you lost for us cut us down to nine thousand dollars. Then I had to cover your training camp expenses and pay off your sparring partners and your trainer and that come to nine thousand easy. So I got nothing left. Come to think of it, I probably lost money getting you where you are today. But look at it this way, Champ. At least we ain't in debt. And I just booked us into a theater down in Cincinnati where they're gonna pay us five thousand dollars a week just for telling the people how we knocked out big Jess Willard."

Dempsey knew he couldn't entirely trust Kearns. He

had suspected for quite some time that his manager played fast and loose with the truth. Kearns loved spending money on liquor and women and there was nothing Jack could do about it.

On July 5, Kearns and Dempsey traveled to Cincinnati to accept a payment of $25,000. All Jack had to do was make an appearance in a park. Dempsey also signed up to tour with the Pantages vaudeville circuit. He was paid an outlandish $15,000 a week.

Jack visited his folks in Salt Lake City. He was upset to hear that his parents wanted to divorce. Jack asked them to try and work things out and they promised to give it another shot. Jack bought his brother, Joe, the taxicab he had always wanted. He gave away more of his money to relatives.

Kearns couldn't wait to tell Jack the good news about the movie deal he had negotiated with a major film company. Dempsey signed the contract immediately. He was given a down payment of $50,000 and 50 percent of the gross. Jack was scheduled to star in a fifteen-episode serial.

The first episode Jack starred in was called *Daredevil Jack*. Dempsey's only concern was the fact that he was scheduled to tour with the circus in twelve weeks and he might not have time to complete every episode. The producer listened to Jack's complaint and assured him he would see what he could do. The director heard about Jack's concern but thought there was no way he could shoot fifteen episodes in just twelve weeks. The producer offered the director a substantial bonus if he could make the deadline. The director accepted the bonus and met the deadline.

In order to make Dempsey more photogenic for the camera, the film company hired Lon Chaney to "overhaul"

Jack's appearance. He applied rouge on his face and added putty on his nose. Chaney saturated Dempsey's hair with a kind of goo.

The hours were long and boring on the set. Jack typically worked from 6:00 am to midnight. He was always conscious about his lack of acting skills. One day he warned the director, W.S. Van Dyke, not to expect a lot out him. "I won't," was Van Dyke's immediate response. Jack had to be taught how to pull a punch because he kept hurting the other actors on the set. The situation got so out of hand, the set's doctor felt compelled to issue a formal complaint against Dempsey.

Kearns and Dempsey agreed on how to split up all the earnings generated from films, the circus, and vaudeville. According to Dempsey, Kearns always divided the money into two piles. Jack received the larger of the two piles. It wasn't until much later when he realized that Kearns always snapped up the pile with the largest denominations.

Dempsey appeared to be living on easy street until one fateful day. He received word that his former wife, Maxine, had written to the editor of a newspaper based in San Francisco. She accused him of being a draft dodger and that he had made several misrepresentations on his draft papers. Moreover, Maxine indicated that she had supported Jack and his family. She claimed she had letters proving her assertions.

As usual, Kearns advised Jack not to worry about it. The public would forget all about his wife's unsubstantiated claims. Such would not be the case, however. The story hit every major newspaper in the country. Organizations were up in arms about Jack's lack of patriotism. Later, Maxine recanted much of her story, but the damage had been done. Dempsey's reputation took a severe beating.

Once again the photographs taken at the Sun Shipyard outside Philadelphia were printed in the newspapers. The word "Slacker" was printed next to Dempsey's name in many newspapers. Jack was afraid that if people associated the word "Slacker" with the name Dempsey, the public at large would begin to believe the accusation. The film company decided not to release *Daredevil Jack,* at least for the time being. Dempsey's bright star was beginning to fade.

The furor over Dempsey's alleged attempt to evade the draft grew ominously worse. On February 27, 1920, a federal grand jury indicted Jack for "unlawfully, willingly, knowingly, and feloniously evading and attempting to evade the draft." As if that wasn't enough, the grand jury issued a bench warrant against Jack.

Kearns was unsure about how all this would play out in terms of Dempsey's career. If he lost Jack, Kearns would suffer alongside his fighter. He knew a champion like Jack Dempsey came along very infrequently. Instead of panicking, Kearns hired who he thought was the best lawyer money could buy. He chose Gavin McNab, a highly successful attorney from San Francisco. McNab offered to take the case for $75,000, with $15,000 down. Kearns was shocked by the enormity of the fee. Too desperate to negotiate for a lower payment, Kearns hired McNab.

An associate of McNab's visited Jack's parents and told them about Jack's case. Dempsey's parents were in the midst of filing for divorce. The associate advised them against this, at least until after their son's court case. It was important for Hyrum and Celia to appear united as a loving couple during the trial.

Kearns sent a friend, Tommy Fitzgerald, to Nevada to try and locate Maxine. Once he found her, Fitzgerald tried to persuade Maxine not to testify against Jack. She told Fitzgerald she would definitely testify against Dempsey in open court. Fitzgerald offered her money not cooperate with the authorities. She agreed to accept the payment in exchange for her promise to hide out in Tijuana until the trial was over.

Kearns accompanied Maxine on her journey. Unbeknownst to Kearns, he was being tailed by federal agents. The agents took Maxine into custody and Kearns got off with a warning not to obstruct justice ever again.

A hearing was called to order on March 20, 1920. Dempsey pleaded not guilty to all charges brought against him. A trial date was set for June 7, 1920, to be held in the U.S. Federal Court in San Francisco before Judge Maurice T. Dooling.

Maxine was called to the stand. She was forced to confess about her aliases and her extramarital affairs with various partners while she was married to Jack. She informed the court that she accepted money in exchange for sex. Incredibly, she claimed that she used some of that money to help support Jack. Dempsey nearly exploded with rage and did everything he could to restrain his anger.

McNab sprung to his feet like a man possessed and shook his fist directly at a beleaguered Maxine. "This is the first time," he bellowed, "since Moses took the laws down from Mt. Sinai, that prostitution is being argued in a court of law as a legitimate means of livelihood!" Maxine was reduced to tears.

McNab asked Maxine how much money her husband sent her in 1917. She wasn't sure. Maybe 500 dollars, more or less. McNab showed Maxine receipts totaling $2,000. Faced with hard evidence proving she had been lying, Maxine broke down. She admitted that the attacks she levied against Dempsey were an attempt to squeeze more money out of him. She desperately needed support.

Dempsey's attorney called more witnesses to the stand. Jack's mother and father were asked to testify on behalf of their son. Jack's mother swore that her son had been and was currently her and Hyrum's sole source of support. She further testified that she allowed Maxine to live in their home and that she taught her how to cook and maintain the household. According to Celia, Maxine was an ingrate and restless and soon took off to parts unknown.

Lt. John F. Kennedy of the Great Lakes Naval Station testified that Jack had wanted to do his part for the Navy. Kearns was also called to the witness stand. He was a bad witness for Jack because he acted defensive and was uncooperative. Dempsey's attorney had called about twenty witnesses in all before he made his closing argument. They all defended Dempsey's claim that he had been the sole support of his wife and parents.

"This boy has done more here in his own country," McNab argued, "in terms of raising money and selling bonds than the ones who are crying foul!"

The jury began their deliberation at 10:30 a.m. on June 15, 1920. They returned with their verdict a mere fifteen minutes later. The foreman, John H. Clendenning, read the verdict out loud. "We, the jury, find William Harrison Dempsey, the defendant at the bar, Not Guilty."

Jack was elated. Tex Rickard and his pal, John Ringling, paid the $75,000 attorney's fee. Rickard later told Jack that the total cost for legal representation totaled $150,000. Kearns thought it was money well spent. He predicted Rickard would make a fortune off of future Dempsey fights.

From that day forward, Jack never saw Maxine again. Over the years, Dempsey heard stories about Maxine's whereabouts and what she was up to. Then in 1924, a fire broke out at a dance hall in Juarez, Mexico. The fire spread to a room above the dance floor where Maxine lay sleeping. Sadly, Maxine perished in the fire.

1920 turned out to be a huge year in sports. Babe Ruth, relinquishing his duties as pitcher for the New York Yankees, smashed an astounding fifty-four home runs. Not only did the Babe hit more home runs than any other player, he swatted more home runs than entire teams. Ruth's very presence almost singlehandedly allowed baseball to survive the 1919 World Series scandal.

In the spring of 1920, Gene Tunney met his idol, Jack Dempsey, on a ferry traveling between Jersey City and Manhattan. The meeting was quite by accident and Tunney took full advantage of the rare opportunity. Tunney hoped that the champion had at least heard of him before he decided to approach Dempsey. Gene walked to where Jack was sitting and introduced himself. The two men exchanged pleasantries. Jack asked how Gene was doing. Tunney informed Dempsey that he was fine except that he had injured his middle knuckle while boxing in France. He added that the knuckle still hadn't healed properly. Dempsey advised Tunney how to tape his knuckles so that when he landed a punch, his injured middle knuckle would absorb less shock. Tunney was moved by Dempsey's friendliness and sympathy and wondered how a ferocious man-killer in the ring could be so friendly and sympathetic outside the ring.

Jack went back to making pictures. He started working at the Hal Roach Studios in Hollywood. Dempsey had the unique opportunity of working with one of the all-time greats, Harold Lloyd. Unfortunately, Lloyd had accidently blown off his thumb and index finger on the set. Production ceased and Jack started work at Brunton Studios.

A circus hired Jack as their main attraction. He was part of a show that included twenty-five wrestlers and several boxers. The show lasted about four weeks and it pulled in an impressive ninety thousand dollars, big money for back then. Jack received fifty percent of the revenue. He was even part of an act involving a Havana cigar smoking chimpanzee.

Dempsey fell head over heels for a beautiful tent performer. Her husband and brother had passed away three years earlier and she turned to Jack for emotional support. Jack's stint with the circus proved to be the happiest time of his life.

Jack wanted to stay with the circus a little longer but Kearns put his foot down. Jack attempted to keep a long-distance relationship going with his friend, but to no avail. His friend explained to Jack that what they had was just a passing fancy. He couldn't figure out why she suddenly acted so aloof toward him. A friend of the lady wrote Jack and explained that she had been paid to end their close relationship.

Jack confronted Kearns about the allegation. Kearns denied any involvement. Dempsey wanted to fire his manager but decided against this drastic measure. He had no real proof other than what somebody had told him. Dempsey may very well have ended their business relationship if it wasn't for the fact that Kearns owed a lot of money to creditors.

Rickard and Kearns decided to go their separate ways. Perhaps Kearns felt that his fighter was so popular, he didn't need an expensive promoter like Rickard. Kearns decided that he would do all the promotion for Jack's fights himself. With the help of another promoter, Floyd Fitzsimmons, Kearns arranged for Dempsey to fight Billy Miske.

Miske and Dempsey were not strangers. On May 3, 1918, they had fought each other in St. Paul, Minnesota. The result of that fight was a ten-round no-decision. Another bout was held on November 28, 1918, in Philadelphia. The fight lasted six rounds and it too ended in a no-decision. His two fights with Dempsey proved that Billy Miske was a very formidable opponent.

Miske had been a close and loyal friend to Jack for years. He had sparred with Jack in an effort to prepare for his battle against the heavyweight champion, Jess Willard. He suffered from serious ailments so grave, he had to be hospitalized. Dempsey was well aware that his friend had health issues. Dempsey was unconcerned about the possible lack of interest in a proposed fight with Billy. Jack was determined to do what he could for his friend and rival.

Dempsey eventually learned that his old friend was apparently in worse shape than he had originally thought. Sources indicated that Miske was dying from Bright's disease. The stricken Miske pleaded with Jack to face him in the ring. He was desperately in need of a huge pay day. It would allow him to pay off all his mounting medical bills. Dempsey immediately agreed to defend his title against Miske.

Many fans bought tickets because they wanted to witness Jack's first title defense. He hadn't fought for well over a year and fans were keenly interested to see if the champ still had the goods. Billy Miske helped sell tickets by declaring that he had never hit the canvas during his entire professional career.

During one of Jack's training sessions, he noticed someone who looked vaguely familiar. It was none other than Tex Rickard. He was wearing a disguise. Rickard had apparently wanted to meet with Jack in secret. He warned Dempsey about how dishonest "Doc" Kearns was.

"Why, that guy has no heartbeat and no blood," Rickard pointed out. "Jack, you just make sure he doesn't do to you what comes naturally to him."

Rickard explained to Jack how devious Kearns was in handling Dempsey's earnings. For two hours Dempsey listened to Rickard's pleadings not to fall for Kearns' duplicity. Jack appreciated Rickard's concern for him. On the other hand, he felt obligated to Kearns for all that he had done for him. They shared a lot of history together and Dempsey didn't want to betray his manager.

Kearns was livid when he learned that Rickard had secretly met with Dempsey. He warned Dempsey never to believe Rickard, that he was not to be trusted under any circumstances. Jack was unsure who to believe at this point. In time, he would find out the hard way just how underhanded Kearns actually was.

Dempsey trained hard for the upcoming fight. He hadn't been in the ring since he slaughtered Willard in 1919.

As always, Kearns hired some of the best sparring partners money could buy. Dempsey sparred with Bill Tate, Panama Joe Gans, Marty Farrell, and the great Harry Greb, also known to the boxing world as the "Pittsburgh Windmill." Greb was one of the most feared fighters in all of boxing.

One day while Dempsey was training, Al Capone paid him a visit. Dempsey recalled that Capone was short and stout and wore a white short-sleeved shirt. Under his wide-brimmed hat he clenched a cigar in his teeth. The mobster didn't allow cameras in the camp. He offered Dempsey a great deal of money just to stage an exhibition in Chicago. Dempsey did not accept the offer. In response, Capone pulled out a huge wad of bills and riffled through them with his thumb. He asked Dempsey if he was impressed. Jack assured Capone that he was very impressed while Big Al waved the huge bankroll under Dempsey's nose.

The day before the scheduled bout, Kearns threatened to cancel the fight. He wanted a friend named Jim Daugherty to act as the referee. Just before fight time the promoter allowed Daugherty to referee the bout. This was the same Jim Daugherty who had hired Dempsey to "work" at the Sun Shipbuilding Company in 1917. Kearns believed that Daugherty could favorably influence the outcome of the bout if it turned out to be close. Kearns left absolutely nothing to chance.

Dempsey struggled over a peculiar dilemma. Should he carry Miske as long as possible so that the fight fans got their money's worth, or should he go for the quick knockout? Jack figured that if he carried the challenger, Miske might get seriously injured. If he knocked him out, Miske could possibly suffer from a severe head injury. Not all was doom and gloom for the challenger, however. He had never been knocked down, let alone knocked out during his entire professional boxing career. He had an outstanding record of 78 professional fights under his belt.

On September 6, 1920, the day of the fight, it was horrifically hot and humid. Dempsey was only an eleven-to-five favorite to retain the heavyweight championship. Billy Miske weighed in at 187 and Dempsey weighed slightly less. The fight was scheduled for ten rounds. If both fighters were on their feet at the end of the bout, a no-decision would be declared. Two of Dempsey's sparring partners fought in a couple preliminary bouts. The once great Sam Langford lost to Bill Tate and Harry Greb handily defeated Chuck Wiggins.

The bell rang to begin the bout. Miske immediately attacked Dempsey with blazing lefts and rights to the head. He was apparently trying to catch the champion off balance. Dempsey responded with a barrage of bombs of his own. He landed several lethal blows to the challenger's head. Jack tried very hard to knock Billy Miske out in the first round, but the challenger was too tough. Miske wouldn't allow Dempsey to tag him on the jaw, so Dempsey concentrated on hammering away at the challenger's body. It suddenly dawned on Kearns that perhaps he had been duped into thinking Miske was seriously ill.

In the second round, Dempsey knocked Miske down. The champ was beginning to find his range. Dempsey continued to stalk Miske, throwing left hooks and rights at Miske's head, but the challenger responded with hard punches of his own. By the time the second round had ended, Kearns feared that Jack was definitely behind on points.

Kearns frantically yelled in Dempsey's ear, "Don't play around with this thing anymore! Look for an opening and finish it quick!"

Jack finally knocked Miske out at 1:13 of the third round. He carried the fallen challenger to his stool amidst loud cheers. But something came over Dempsey at that exact moment. He was sickened by the cheers while his friend lay motionless. At that key moment he felt ashamed to be a boxer.

Dempsey was harshly criticized after the fight for beating a sick man. Miske, however, went on to fight such highly regarded heavyweights as Fred Fulton, Bill Brennan, and the very cagey but clumsy Willie Meehan. Amazingly, Miske went on to defeat nearly every opponent he faced, twenty-four in all, until his death in 1924.

"I tried to knock him out in the first round," Jack recounted years later, "but the best I could do was hurt him with a body punch. I couldn't get a shot at his jaw. In the second round I got a part of it and knocked him down. In the third round, I just shut my eyes, hit him with a left that straightened him up, then let the right hand go – and that's all there was to it. I carried Billy to his stool and nearly got sick to my stomach while the two seconds worked on him bringing him to. I had forgotten the boos before the fight and now I couldn't hear the cheers for me, cheers that always came after one. The crowd was very excited and as a matter of fact, it had been an exciting fight."

The gate totaled a paltry $134,904. Kearns and Dempsey earned $55,000 in a little over seven minutes of ring action. Kearns received two thirds of the purse and Jack received the balance. Their share of the purse was by far their largest payout ever. Billy Miske gratefully accepted a payment of $25,000 for the fight.

Soon after the Dempsey-Miske slaughter, eight White Sox baseball players were indicted by a Chicago grand jury. The jury determined that gamblers and Chicago White Sox players, or the Chicago Eight as they were fondly referred to, conspired to throw the World Series, thus allowing the Cincinnati Reds to win. Many of the players rationalized their behavior by claiming they were underpaid for their extraordinary services.

Ring Lardner, the cynical but hugely popular sportswriter, smelled a rat immediately while watching the World Series. While many sportswriters believed the White Sox, by far the best team in all of baseball, were simply playing bad baseball, Lardner believed something sinister had occurred in the Series. Lardner even wrote some humorous lyrics describing his feelings toward the alleged scandal. The song is a parody to the tune, "I'm Forever Blowing Bubbles."

> I'm forever blowing ball games,
> Pretty ball games in the air,
> I come from Chi.,
> I hardly try,
> Just go to bat and fade and die,
> Fortune's coming my way,
> That's why I don't care,
> I'm forever blowing ball games,
> For the gamblers treat me fair.

Many will argue that after the scandal broke, Americans who followed baseball desperately needed a hero. By and large, baseball players were no longer trusted and idolized by the American public. Sports fans craved something or someone to idolize. Many Americans, including Ring Lardner himself, turned to Jack Dempsey as the answer to their wishes and prayers. What they saw Dempsey do to Willard in the ring was real and genuine. No sane champion would have allowed himself to be slaughtered, maimed, and thoroughly humiliated in the ring for the sake of some underhanded payoff. No, Dempsey was now America's new hero. But he would soon become more than that. He would become America's first mega sports hero. Even Babe Ruth worshiped Dempsey. Ruth seriously contemplated becoming a prize fighter because he was in awe of Dempsey's greatness in the ring and all the adulation Jack received from the public.

Kearns and Dempsey were mobbed wherever they went. In the interest of saving time, Kearns tried to convince Dempsey to provide a copy of his autograph on photographs instead of taking the time to sign each photograph himself. To his credit, Jack refused to fake his signature.

Boxing was a highly controversial sport prior to the 1920s. Pugilism was vilified by fanatical religious organizations throughout America. Prominent businessmen like Major Anthony Drexel Biddle of Main Line Philadelphia, however, spoke about what he believed were the virtues of boxing. He tried in vain to encourage politicians to introduce legislation favorable to boxing.

James J. Walker, the gifted senator from the state of New York, was not afraid to vigorously promote boxing. His attitude toward the fight game may have been influenced by his upbringing. He grew up in the rough and tumble Irish section of Greenwich Village. Walker success-fully helped pass legislation to legalize boxing in the New York legislature.

Walker's battle was far from over, however. He still needed the governor's blessing. That man was none other than Alfred Smith. Smith, an Irish Catholic, knew only too well that his political enemies would try to crush him if he signed the bill. His critics warned sympathetic politicians and the public alike that Smith was bent on legalizing box-ing and ending prohibition. Smith recognized that boxing had an unsavory past in his state. Many folks remembered the days when boxing was controlled by crooked gamblers and dishonest fight managers and promoters.

Walker approached Smith about signing the bill, but the governor remained unmoved. He didn't want to risk his political future over a bill which allowed men to beat each other up for a living. Walker tried to convince Smith that the bill addressed important issues, such as ensuring unsal-aried commissioners and strict punishment against anyone circumventing any of the rules.

Smith remained unconvinced by Walker's arguments. The governor provided Walker with a ray of hope when he indicated he would sign the bill into law under one condi-tion. Walker needed to provide Smith with one hundred letters from Protestant clergymen who supported the bill by early Monday morning. That very morning, Smith was appalled to see on his desk hundreds of telegrams from men of the cloth. That same day, Governor Al Smith signed into law the boxing bill and a beer bill.

In between bouts, Dempsey toured with the Pantages vaudeville circuit. While touring with the circuit, Jack met a young magician named Harry Houdini. Dempsey found Houdini to be very cordial and professional. The magician displayed brilliant playing card mastery and magical stunts. Houdini never divulged any of his secrets to anyone, not even to Dempsey. Houdini tried to sell Kearns a concoction of his called "Kickapoo Elixir" for a dollar. Kearns refused his offer. He did, however, try to sell Houdini his own special concoction. Dempsey enjoyed working the vaudeville circuit. It was hard work but Jack didn't seem to mind.

Jack continued to suffer from the stigma of avoiding the draft. Although the war had been over for two years, much of the public still held a grudge against his alleged refusal to join the military. The "slacker" charge would continue to haunt him for the rest of his career.

Kearns arranged for Dempsey to defend his title against a very tough opponent, Bill Brennan. The fight was scheduled to take place in the old Madison Square Garden in New York. This marked the second time these extraordinary fighters would face each other in the ring. Jack was annoyed to hear from several sources that Brennan probably would have defeated him in their last fight if the challenger hadn't broken his ankle. On the other hand, Kearns and Dempsey understood that this type of controversy might beef up the gate.

Bill Brennan had sixty fights under his belt. The rough, tough Brennan had only lost four contests, one of them by knockout. Brennan's real name was William Shanks. He was of German decent and he was born in Louisville, Kentucky. He changed his name shortly before the start of World War I. He may have changed his name due to the fact that many Americans despised Germans during and after the war.

"Doc" Kearns was under the impression that "there were sinister influences at work to try to take the title away from us." Kearns suspected Brennan was under the thumb of mobsters. He feared some sort of "gangland betting coup" was being hatched. Dempsey was a four-to-one favorite and Kearns thought the mob could clean up if they bet on Brennan to win and Jack lost the title.

Tickets for the fight went for anywhere between twenty-five dollars to two dollars. The fight was an immediate sellout. Madison Square Garden managed to accommodate 16,948 die-hard fight fans. The *New York Times* reported that "Everybody wants to see the slashing, tearing title-holder." The Garden first opened for business on June 16, 1890. Concerts showcasing classical music were very common. Auto shows, boat shows, bicycle races, dog shows and many other various types of entertainment soon followed.

Dempsey had a great deal of respect for Bill Brennan. He thought Brennan possessed the same kind of courage all the great champions had. He believed Brennan shared the same conviction John L. Sullivan, Gentleman Jim Corbett, and Bob Fitzsimmons held, in that they could beat anyone in the ring.

Dempsey trained at the Van Kelton Tennis Courts on Fifty-seventh Street and Eighth Avenue. He reportedly trained on the *Granite State* as well. The ship was docked at Ninety-sixth Street. Dempsey trained exceedingly hard for the second defense of his title. Unfortunately, the fight was postponed for several weeks. Jack later claimed he had become stale because he continued to train hard right up until the day of the fight.

Dempsey believed he made a horrible mistake by

training in New York City. He really wanted to train in the country where the air was clean. He missed chopping wood in order to build his "choppy" muscles. He concluded later that he was exercising the same muscles over and over again. Had he trained in the country, he would have experienced "varied, all-around outdoor activities."

Jack thought there were many physical similarities between himself and the challenger. Going into the fight, Brennan weighed 190 pounds and Jack was one pound lighter. They both stood at six feet one and a half inches. Their wrists and ankles and necks measured exactly the same. Jack's reach was 78 inches and Brennan's was only one inch shorter. Surprisingly, Jack was not able to draw large crowds at any of his training sessions. Al Jolson was asked to put on some shows in order to draw more people to the camp.

As was customary, the challenger entered the ring first. Brennan wore a worn red sweater and green boxing trunks, a reference to his supposed ancestral country, Ireland. Dempsey followed the challenger shortly afterwards. He entered the ring wearing his usual long white shorts. This time, however, he decided not to wear his customary robe. Instead, he wore a white towel draped over his taut shoulders.

The champ looked like a predator ready to devour some hapless, unsuspecting prey. He glanced out at the audience, occasionally nodding to an appreciative fan. "Doc" Kearns recalled later that his fighter's "legs were shaking when he came into the Garden ring that night." He attributed Jack's condition not to nervousness but instead to womanizing the night before. According to Kearns, Dempsey was in the worst condition of his entire career. At least one person disagreed with Kearns. A reporter for the *New York Times* wrote that "the lightly drawn skin over the champion's cheekbones and the clear look in his deep-set eyes and his general calm and steadiness proved that Dempsey had worked and worked hard to attain that perfection of condition which has always stood him in good stead."

The crowd booed Dempsey the moment he stepped into the ring at ten-thirty p.m. The catcalls bothered Jack tremendously, but he also had a much more pressing issue on his mind. He knew Bill Brennan was about to give him a great deal of difficulty in the ring. Although many boxing experts thought that Brennan was live bait, Jack knew a lot better. Dempsey had always been concerned about being hammered by a hard blow to the jaw, and Brennan was fully capable of doing just that. Dempsey's style was built off the notion that one lucky punch from an opponent is all it took to lose a fight. He reasoned, therefore, that the best defense was a good offence. His ring philosophy explains why so many of his fights ended in the first round.

Dempsey had difficulty landing punches in round one. Brennan had a powerful right hand as well as a long, vicious left. He effectively side stepped many of Jack's punches. In the second round, Brennan smashed a hard right to Jack's chin, causing him to stagger. For several seconds, Jack felt extremely vulnerable. He recalled after the fight that if Brennan had only followed up after seriously hurting him, the challenger may very well have won the title right then and there. One can justifiably argue that a key difference between a great boxer and a good boxer is that the former takes full advantage of opportunities that suddenly present themselves. Brennan allowed Dempsey to recuperate from a vicious beating. After that round, Dempsey could only remember Kearns screaming hysterically that he was losing the fight and he needed a knockout in order to win.

One reporter said it best when he wrote that the "champion seemed bewildered when he was repeatedly unable to reach Brennan after charging in with a lightning-like shift. He seemed worried. Brennan's long slinging left bothered him. The champion seemed at sea as to how to avoid it, and try as he might he was unable to drive his powerful rights and lefts to a vital spot. He was not the Dempsey who has been accustomed to lay his opponents low in two or three rounds."

Another reporter from the *New York Times* wrote that "It looked for a moment as if Dempsey would go crashing to the floor and be counted out. Brennan seemed surprised. He stepped back to look the champion over. Bill could hardly believe his eyes. He didn't seem to be able to grasp the fact that he had the champion in a dangerous way. That brief hesitation enabled Dempsey to regain his scattered senses. Dempsey quickly stepped into a clinch and when the referee finally succeeded in prying him loose, he had so far recovered that he was able to fight back and was giving Brennan as good as he received when the bell sounded and ended the round."

Dempsey soon recognized for the first time that he had slowed down considerably. His punches were no longer lightning fast and his reflexes had deteriorated. The next several rounds belonged to Brennan. The challenger threw punches at Dempsey from all angles. Brennan was methodically wearing the champion down to the point of exhaustion.

In the tenth round, Brennan landed a hard right on Dempsey's ear, causing it to bleed profusely. The blow actually severed part of Jack's ear from the base. Jack became exceedingly alarmed because he thought his ear was hanging off of his head. He feared that one more haymaker might rip his ear off. Brennan kept pounding at Dempsey's torn ear the best he could, hoping perhaps that Dempsey would panic at the thought of losing his ear entirely. The thought of ending up with a cauliflower ear, a badge of honor for some boxers, probably struck fear and panic in Dempsey's heart. A ringside reporter noted that "Dempsey was white and ghastly with rage as he glared at Brennan from his stool."

Kearns reminded Dempsey that he needed to knock Brennan out in order to keep the title. Jack was determined not to lose his title at all costs. The very thought of losing after holding the title for only one year was more than he could bear. He had to defeat Brennan with an all-out, no prisoners assault that even the very skillful challenger could not defend against.

In the eleventh round, Dempsey swarmed all over Brennan with hard rights and left hooks to the body. For the first time in the fight, Brennan looked dazed and hurt. Near the end of the round, the challenger almost dropped to the canvas but managed to survive the round.

Kearns gave Dempsey hell for fighting so lethargically against the very same fighter he convincingly beat just four years ago. "You're supposed to be the heavyweight champion of the world and you're stinkin' out the joint, you creep. You've thrown it all away because of a cheap broad. If you got any guts left at all you'll pull up your socks and go out there and belt this bum out!"

In the twelfth round, Brennan landed a hard punch to Dempsey's torn and bloody ear. Jack hammered Brennan's face with a hard right. He landed a hard left to Brennan's stomach, followed by a right hook to the heart. Brennan dropped to the canvas in excruciating agony. As he tried to rise from the canvas, Dempsey strolled over to him, ready to pounce like a wild beast. Brennan was counted out as he struggled to his feet. Dempsey always asserted that his second bout with Tunney and his second meeting with Brennan were by far his toughest fights. Grantland Rice wrote that with an ear that "looked like a cross between a veal cutlet breaded and a sponge dipped in gore," Jack walked back to his corner, thoroughly exhausted and grateful that he had retained for a second time the world's heavyweight title.

After the bout, ring announcer Joe Humphreys stepped into the ring. Humphreys was blessed with a booming voice that could clearly be heard far up into the rafters. He refused to use a megaphone, calling anyone who did so a "sissy." Tex Rickard stood alongside Humphreys as the ring announcer presented a diamond-studded belt signifying the world heavyweight championship to a very deserving and exhausted Jack Dempsey.

Brennan visited Dempsey in the champion's dressing room after his devastating loss. "It took you twice as long this time, you lucky stiff," Brennan joked. "It's my turn, next. Out you go."

The gate grossed an impressive $208,000. The total included newsreel rights of the fight. Kearns and Dempsey earned $100,000 for the fight. They also received $8,000 from the movies. Brennan received $35,000.

One New York newspaper referred to the fight as

"one of the most vicious and closely contested heavyweight bouts ever seen." John Wray, a reporter for the *St. Louis Post Dispatch,* noted that "Dempsey is no superman." He indicated in his column that adulation toward the champion "had been over-played to the point of near-in-fallibility." Many fight fans agreed with Wray in his analysis of Dempsey's vulnerabilities, but many more fans still believed in Dempsey's prowess in the ring. The slaughter he bestowed upon Willard was still fresh in the minds of many sports fans.

The fight proved beyond a reasonable doubt that Dempsey was not invincible in the ring. Had Jack been as superhuman as many fight fans believed, as evidenced by his amazing victory over Jess Willard, he would not have come close to losing to Brennan, a man he had discharged after only six rounds in an earlier contest. But the fight also proved that Dempsey could withstand ferocious blows to the jaw and then only seconds later stalk his opponent with a vengeance.

Gene Tunney, who had been present at the fight, was awestruck by the way Dempsey put Brennan away. He was impressed by the sheer punishment Dempsey bestowed upon Brennan's body. Tunney, however, was just as impressed by Dempsey's lack of adequate defensive skills. He also noticed that whenever Jack threw wild punches, thus leaving himself open, Brennan did not take advantage of those moments. Tunney was under the impression that a boxer shrewder than Brennan could possibly beat Dempsey.

The two fighters almost had a return match, but it was not to be. They were scheduled to fight in Michigan City a year after their bout in New York. Michigan's governor

Vintage photo of early 20th century American boxer "Fireman" Jim Flynn (1879-1935). Flynn (real name Andrew Chiariglione) twice fought for the World Heavyweight Championship — losing to Tommy Burns in 1906 and to Jack Johnson in 1912. He is also famous for knocking out future heavyweight champion Jack Dempsey in 1917 — the only man ever to do so.

Jack with his dog on a ranch in Colorado.

Jack Dempsey fights Tommy Gibbons
in Shelby, Montana, July 1923.

Luis Firpo knocks Jack Dempsey through the ropes into the press row where he landed on a reporter's typewriter. Dempsey got back in the ring and stopped Firpo with two knockdowns in the second round.

Jack Dempsey about 1925.

Jack Dempsey and his wife, Estelle Taylor, rehearse their lines for the stage production of 'The Big Fight,' 1928.

Jack Dempsey's famous crouching attack in the fourth round of his bout against Gene Tunney, Sept. 23, 1926. Tunney won the boxing match.

'Long Count Fight', the Gene Tunney-Jack Dempsey boxing
match of Sept. 22, 1927. Jack Dempsey (dark trunks)
batters Tunney against the ropes in the 7th round
until he falls.

put a halt to the fight, apparently because the slacker charge against Dempsey was a real deal killer in that state. Something much more serious and sinister occurred that put an end to any chance of a future bout between them. Several years later, Bill Brennan was executed gangland style. He was the proud owner of a Chicago based speakeasy, but he made the fatal mistake of buying beer from the "wrong" gangland supplier.

"Doc" Kearns decided that Dempsey's next opponent should be Georges Carpentier, the French light heavyweight champion. Carpentier was ruggedly handsome, charismatic, and he had served in the French military. In essence, the Frenchman was a national war hero.

On October 12, 1920, Carpentier faced Battling Levinsky in a twelve-round bout in Jersey City, New Jersey for the light heavyweight title. Carpentier easily annihilated the champion, knocking out Levinsky in the fourth round. The referee claimed after the bout that he had never witnessed a punch as devastating as the one Carpentier displayed in his fight against Levinsky. Levinsky's manager, Dan Morgan, was so impressed with Carpentier's punching ability, he indicated that Carpentier should have no problem knocking out the reigning heavyweight champion. "I tell you those terrible punches to the jaw will knock out Jack Dempsey," Morgan claimed. "He will knock him cold," he confidently predicted.

Not everyone was excited about Georges Carpentier's prospects as the next heavyweight champion. Herbert Reed, columnist for the *Evening Post*, wrote that "Compared with Dempsey at the moment, he left the impression of being just a remarkable amateur." Alfred W. McGann of the *Globe* went so far as to write that "It was no contest. It was a setup. Levinsky went into the ring to get the money."

Georges Carpentier had been a courageous aviator during the war and he was a highly decorated French ace. He began boxing at a very early age as a bantamweight. As he grew stronger he fought as a lightweight and then as a middleweight. He eventually fought as a light-heavyweight. He was known for his amazing speed and could knock opponents out with powerful blows. According to Dempsey, Carpentier possessed an effective, devastating weapon. Jack referred to the punch as a "sort of Mary Ann in reverse, that came down from the sky instead of up from the floor." In short, it was a looping, overhand swing that stunned and terrified many an opponent in the ring.

The fight contract had actually been signed by Dempsey and Carpentier one month prior to the Dempsey-Brennan fight. Carpentier's manager, Francois Deschamps, told newspaper reporters that his fighter would only meet Dempsey in the ring once Jack's military issues were resolved.

As soon as Carpentier arrived in America he was mobbed by throngs of admirers, particularly young women. He wore tailor-made suits and silk shirts. The American public fell in love with the young, dashing Frenchman. On May 30, 1921, Carpentier and his entourage visited President Theodore Roosevelt's memorial. Later that day, he witnessed several boxing bouts in Brooklyn and drew huge crowds of people who came just to get a glimpse of the new French boxing sensation.

According to Dempsey, Carpentier never allowed anyone other than his entourage near him while he was being weighed. This was probably due to the fact that he weighed quite a bit less than Dempsey. He didn't want the word to get out that perhaps he was not a formidable enough challenger for Dempsey.

The press was not permitted anywhere near the Frenchman's training camp. Ring Lardner was so upset about being shunned, he wrote an article about the episode. He sarcastically suggested that perhaps Carpentier was "practicing his ten second nap."

Dempsey's training camp was the exact opposite of Carpentier's. Everyone was allowed to watch Dempsey spar, pull weights, and shadowbox as long as they paid two bits. Jack had absolutely nothing to hide. He was grateful his fight with Brennan had been long and brutal. He understood that the fight allowed him to get in the kind of shape he needed to be in against a dangerous opponent like Carpentier.

The challenger set up camp in Manhasset, New York. Rumors spread that Carpentier had developed and improved a "secret" punch that could win the fight for him. To a certain degree, Carpentier had utilized a similar punch against men much bigger than him. It was a hard, quick punch, commonly known in the boxing world as a "sneaky right hand" punch. Carpentier was almost certain that this one weapon alone could very well even the playing field between him and Dempsey. Carpentier's legs were exceedingly strong and muscular. They helped the Frenchman spring out of a crouch so that he could throw his right more effectively.

Dempsey paid little or no attention to all the deals made behind closed doors. He trusted Kearns' judgement and expertise regarding negotiations between Rickard and Kearns. His job was to destroy Carpentier and nothing else. Dempsey put on such an exhibition of his unique fighting skills that Bill Brennan was heard to have said that "Dempsey will knock Carpentier out before the fourth round." Jack characteristically spared no one in the ring during his brutal, take no prisoners sparring sessions. Light heavyweight "Battling" Gahee battled to stay on his feet against the Manassa Mauler. Dempsey loosened Gahee's teeth and knocked him down inside two rounds of sparring. The beatings were so brutal, Dempsey asked Kearns to raise the wages for all the sparring partners.

The champ began training in earnest in April at a health farm in Long Hill, New Jersey. The farm was owned by Freddie Welsh, the former lightweight champion. He had lost his title to the great Benny Leonard. Dempsey decided early on to spar against men much lighter than him in order to improve his speed. He sparred with the likes of Alex Trambidas, Joe Benjamin, and Jimmy Darcy. Kearns moved Jack's training camp to Atlantic City in May. Dempsey gratefully accepted the change. He relished the openness of the resort town. He enjoyed swimming in the ocean and even claimed that the rough surf helped further develop his muscles.

Carpentier also demonstrated his ability to give sparring partners a thrashing. He actually knocked out a fighter he had difficulty with in an earlier match in Paris. That fighter was the highly respected Joe Jeannette. Some cynics claimed, however, that the "knock out" was probably just a publicity stunt in order to bolster Carpentier's image. A novel but effective method of training was utilized in order to improve Carpentier's speed in the ring. Rabbits were set loose in and around the training camp and the Frenchman's job was to chase them down.

Several weeks before the match, Dempsey and Carpentier played a round of golf together. Carpentier spoke just enough English to be able to make a veiled threat to Dempsey about their upcoming fight.

"I hope," Carpentier said to Jack, "we will still be friends after the fight."

The bout was scheduled for July 2, 1921, at a place called Boyle's Thirty Acres near Jersey City, New Jersey. Kearns had proven that he was ineffective as a promoter and so he allowed Tex Rickard to promote the fight. Rickard wanted to stage the fight at the Polo Grounds in New York, but the governor imposed too many regulations. Political boss Frank Hague ensured Rickard that the fight could take place in New Jersey.

Rickard offered Kearns a percentage of the gate. Kearns had accepted the offer but later changed his mind. He agreed to a fixed payment of $300,000. Carpentier agreed to be paid $200,000 with no percentage of the gate. According to Dempsey, Kearns' agreement cost the pair about $150,000.

Rickard believed the best way to sell the fight to the public was to accentuate Carpentier's war record and at the same time, remind the public about Dempsey's slacker allegations. Jack was shocked to discover that Kearns had encouraged negative publicity against his fighter just to build up the gate.

Rickard originally built an arena that held 50,000 seats. It was soon determined that more seats were needed and the number rose to 70,000. Later, more seats were built due to the enormous publicity the fight generated.

The Dempsey-Carpentier fight became the first million-dollar gate. The fight broke many other records as well. The fight would draw the largest crowd ever to witness a sporting event. It would become the first world title fight ever to be broadcast via the radio. Reportedly, the first fight to be broadcast via radio was held just a few months earlier. Westinghouse's KDKA broadcast the Johnny Dundee-Johnny Ray lightweight fight from Pittsburgh's Motor Square Garden.

Many of the celebrities who came to see the "Fight of the Century" included William H. Vanderbilt, Henry Ford, Vincent Astor, George M. Cohan, Colonel Jacob Ruppert, owner of the New York Yankees, Flo Ziegfeld, Harry Sinclair, the oil king, and the ever popular Al Jolson.

New York Times reporter Irvin S. Cobb wrote that the "arts, the sciences, the drama, commerce, politics, the bar, the great newly risen industry of bootlegging — all these have been sent their pink, their pick and their perfection to grace this great occasion. A calling over of the names of the occupants of the more highly priced reservations would sound like reading the first hundred pages of Who's Ballyhoo in America." Tex Rickard quipped that "If it takes all sorts to make up the world, the world must be here already."

Not everything went smoothly, however. Several fans had to be cared for in the arena's emergency hospital because of heat exhaustion. During a preliminary bout, a spectator became dangerous to those around him and had to be escorted to the emergency hospital. In the process, he bit a hospital attendant and attacked a doctor.

93,000 boxing fans came to see the fight. Unfortunately, the arena swayed under the weight of all those people. Police and fire officials begged Rickard to begin the fight sooner than previously scheduled. One man screamed: "Everybody stay down! You're in a dangerous place! The paraphernalia is wheeling! Everybody down!" He then turned his attention to a nearby police officer and yelled, "If you police can't make them sit down, club them down!"

Rickard barged into Jack's dressing room. "Jack! Jack! You never seen anything like it. We got a million dollars in already and they're still coming!" Rickard calmed down enough to warn Dempsey not to destroy Carpentier too early in the fight.

"Give the people out there a good run for their money, but be careful. Don't kill him. Don't kill everything. Give the people what they came for. If you kill him, boxing will be dead."

Dempsey simply nodded and shrugged his shoulders in response to Rickard's suggestion. He knew only too well that any fighter was capable of landing a devastating punch to the jaw and he was not about to provide that opportunity to Carpentier. He had been in enough fights to recognize that he could not afford to give any opponent a break. Dempsey knew Rickard was only thinking about his own self-interest as a promoter.

According to Kearns, Rickard warned Dempsey not to "mess it up." Kearns demanded clarification. Rickard expressed his concern that Jack should not knock the Frenchman out with one punch in the first round. Kearns told Rickard to tell Carpentier "not to run and nothing will be messed up because we'll give you a helluva fight."

Rickard, not sure if he had made his point, nevertheless hurried out of the dressing room. Kearns sternly warned Jack not to take Rickard's suggestions seriously. "Don't pay no attention to that malarkey," he warned his fighter. "You go out there and knock this guy flat as quick as possible. We don't carry nobody. I don't give a damn if you break him in half. Knock him out just as quick as you damn well can."

Six preliminary bouts were featured prior to the main event. Gene Tunney, fighting as a light-heavyweight, faced a rough-around-the edges fighter who went by the name of Soldier Jones. Tunney knocked his opponent out in the seventh round. He displayed some remarkable boxing savvy, but he was far from the Gene Tunney the world would come to idolize a few years hence.

The Dempsey-Carpentier fight was deemed a "no-decision" fight according to New Jersey law. In other words, Dempsey could lose the fight only by being knocked out or if he landed a disqualifying low blow to Carpentier. By fight time, Dempsey was a 2-to-1 favorite, surprisingly low odds considering the champion appeared to be invincible against a much smaller opponent. The odds may have reflected the distain many still felt toward Dempsey because of his lack of military involvement.

Fight time for the main event finally arrived. Dempsey slipped into his maroon sweater and headed toward the ring. He looked ferocious as he brushed by lines of admiring fans. He was greeted with cheers as he stepped into the ring. There were those who were not so kind.

"Slacker! Get outta there, ya bum!" could be heard as well.

Angry spectators threatened to tear Jack's boxing trunks off because sewn on Dempsey's waistband was the

American flag. Dempsey was upset by their threats. He had some difficulty trying to focus all his attention on his opponent. Carpentier was greeted with cheers as he entered the ring. Fist fights broke out between overzealous Dempsey and Carpentier fans.

The ring announcer, Joe Humphreys, stood in the center of the ring and yelled out instructions for the main event. When Dempsey's name was announced, the crowd let out a tremendous roar. The crowd went wild when Humphreys yelled out Carpentier's name. Dempsey had weighed in at 188 pounds and Carpentier weighted in at 175 pounds. Jack noticed the challenger appeared skinnier than he had expected.

Kearns gave Jack one last bit of advice just before the beginning of the first round. "Remember," Kearns advised Dempsey, "don't take no chances with this guy. Belt him out as quick as you can." Dempsey nodded in agreement.

The bell rang and the two fighters met near the center of the ring. They circled one another, each studying the other's style of boxing. Dempsey fought cautiously at first in round one. He quickly developed an idea about the Frenchman's style of boxing. About halfway through the round, Dempsey landed some hard punches that sent Carpentier smashing against the ropes. Whenever the challenger tried to tie Dempsey up in a clinch, Jack simply freed one arm and pounded Carpentier's body. As the round ended, Carpentier's torso was beet red from Dempsey's blows. Realizing Dempsey could quite possibly win the fight through sheer strength and stamina, the challenger tried to end the fight early by suddenly lunging at Jack with a hard right to the jaw. Jack simply shook off the blow. W.O. McGeehan wrote that the challenger's punches were shells "bursting against an impenetrable armor plate."

In the second round, Carpentier caught Dempsey on the chin with a hard right. The blow staggered Jack. He was amazed how hard Carpentier could punch. Carpentier, however, failed to follow through with more blistering blows. Jack later learned that the challenger had broken his thumb from the blow. The crowd screamed as the underdog hammered the champion with vicious lefts and rights. It appeared to many in the audience that Carpentier might actually win the bout. Indeed, writer W.J. Macbeth indicated that Carpentier was making a "veritable monkey of the champion." Dempsey thought otherwise, however. He believed Carpentier shared the same sentiment. Carpentier stunned Jack with a straight overhand right to Jack's jaw. This round proved to the Frenchman's only real chance of pulling off a huge upset. As Dempsey headed back to his corner, he heard ringsiders yelling up at him. "What's the matter, slacker? The Frenchman too tough for you? Maybe you're all washed up!"

Sportswriter Heywood Broun chimed in that the challenger was definitely "within a punch of the championship." Other influential writers were not so taken in by Carpentier's attempt to unseat Dempsey. Cynic H.L. Mencken fervently believed that "Dempsey was never in any more danger of being knocked out than I was, sitting there in the stands with a pretty gal just behind me and five or six just in front." Mencken harshly criticized the notion that the Frenchman had any chance at all against the champion. The claim that Carpentier could possibly win was "apocryphal, bogus, hollow and null, imbecile, devoid of substance." After the second round, the chances of Carpentier winning the title were soon dashed by the hard, cold reality of Jack Dempsey's apparent invincibility inside the ring.

In the third round, Dempsey came out swinging, apparently trying to end the fight. He hammered away at Carpentier's face with lethal blows. He landed a hard blow to the challenger's stomach, causing the Frenchman to cover up. As the two fighters walked back to their corner at the end of a very brutal round, the crowd grew quieter. Perhaps they sensed that the end was fast approaching for Carpentier. "Doc" Kearns advised Dempsey to end the fight.

"Go to it, kid. Get him now!"

In the fourth round, Dempsey swarmed all over his victim. He landed several blows to Carpentier's horribly bruised body. Dempsey smashed Carpentier with a vicious left hook and the challenger hit the canvas in agony. As soon as the referee reached the count of eight, Carpentier sprang to his feet as if he had been playing possum.

Carpentier threw several more punches at Dempsey but the champ blocked them. Finally, Jack landed several more lefts and then a brutal right and Carpentier crashed to the canvas a second time. The Frenchman tried valiantly to get up before being counted out at 1:16 of the fourth and final round. Dempsey rushed over to the fallen challenger and helped him to his feet. Carpentier was bleeding profusely from his nose and mouth.

And so the "Battle of the Century" proved instead to be the "Promotion of the Century." The entire fight proved to be almost totally one-sided. The fight's buildup turned out to be the most successful aspect of this hugely popular sporting event. If anyone's talents truly shined, it was Tex Rickard's promotional genius.

Newspapers throughout the land heaped praise upon Dempsey. The *New York Times* devoted the first dozen or so pages to the fight. No other sports figure in history had ever been given this much press. Not everyone, however, praised Dempsey's brutality in the ring and Carpentier's courage in the face of almost certain defeat. America's so-called moralists and religious leaders viciously attacked the bout as outrageously immoral. From the pulpit, Dr. John Roach Straton claimed that the fight was an indication that "we have elapsed into paganism." Amazingly, he was most concerned that women and more importantly, little impressionable girls were exposed to "half-naked men."

After the fight, Carpentier granted the American press an interview to discuss the bout. He used an interpreter because he knew very little English. "Dempsey is a fearful puncher," the Frenchman proclaimed. "Every blow he landed on my body hurt me terribly. But the American people were told that I am game and courageous and I could not disappoint them any more than I could disappoint the people of France. I would not throw in the towel. The fight could end only as it did — with a knockout. I salute Jack Dempsey, the greatest boxer I have ever faced, the greatest boxer in the world."

Dempsey had much to say about the challenger as well. "Carpentier is a great fighter himself," Dempsey remarked. "He took his medicine without a whimper. I intend to give every logical candidate a chance to fight me, and if the public wants me to meet Georges again, I will. But I really think he's just too light to beat me. He's a great light heavyweight champion and from here on he ought to prove that by taking on the best in that class."

Gene Tunney learned something very important that day. The lesson learned would help him immensely in his quest for the heavyweight championship title. He noticed, in his view, a significant flaw in Dempsey's fighting ability. For some inexplicable reason, Dempsey was vulnerable to a simple right cross. It may have been partially due to the fact that he was a lethal slugger who possessed only rudimentary boxing skills. In Jack's mind, perhaps, he didn't need to be an exceptional boxer because he could destroy opponents with both fists. This could explain why he never developed an effective defensive maneuver against the right cross.

Over the next several years, Boyle's Thirty Acres would be the home for many spectacular fights. A year after the Dempsey- Carpentier bout, Benny Leonard would go on to defeat Lew Tendler in a title fight. In July, 1923, Luis Angel Firpo would destroy Jess Willard by knocking the ex-champion out in the eighth round. Tex Rickard was forced to dismantle the historic arena because New York City was fast becoming the boxing mecca of the entire world.

CHAPTER SIX

THE BOXER AND THE WILD BULL

Dempsey successfully defends his title against the "Wild Bull of the Pampas" in one of the most controversial title fights ever.

Tex Rickard and Jack Kearns seriously considered staging a Dempsey-Willard rematch. The proposed bout would probably be held at Boyle's Thirty Acres on July 1, 1922. Kearns had some reservations, however. He felt that Willard might not want to risk another brutal thrashing. Of course, any fighter might consider facing Dempsey as long as the price was right. Rumors surfaced suggesting that Jess Willard was having second thoughts about fighting the champion because he was doing considerably well with many of his oil investments.

Kearns advised Dempsey that he should take it easy for a while. Rickard totally agreed with Kearns. Speaking from strictly a financial point of view, Rickard thought that overexposure might hurt future gates. Rickard wanted Jack to fight only once a year. Dempsey, however, was not sold on the idea. He enjoyed fighting and he didn't want to be sidelined for any length of time.

Jack Kearns was of the opinion that because the competition in the heavyweight division at that time was weak, Dempsey should not fight. He was well aware of the fact that Dempsey would probably be criticized for "ducking" certain fighters who may have been deemed worthy enough for a chance to face Jack in the ring. Kearns wanted to provide the public with a "spectacular fight," not just a slaughter.

Kearns proudly compared Jack Dempsey to Babe Ruth in the sense that both sports figures created an "air of anticipation" and excitement. You never knew when Dempsey might suddenly explode with an attack so fierce, it could send a challenger to the canvas. Fans admired Ruth's uncanny ability to suddenly send a ball whistling over the heads of amazed spectators for a yet another tape measure home run.

Dempsey and Kearns tried making money in the investment world. Unfortunately, success in the fight business didn't transfer very well to other types of businesses. In no time at all the pair lost $75,000 investing in coal property in Utah.

Dempsey and Kearns visited Europe. Jack was treated like royalty wherever he went. He was extremely self-conscious of his appearance while in the company of nobility. He even tried wearing a monocle in order to look more dignified. Kearns told him he looked like an ass and so Jack never wore the eye piece again. While in Paris, the Parisian government proudly bestowed Dempsey with a medal of honor. Apparently, the French people didn't harbor any ill will toward Dempsey for knocking out their beloved Georges Carpentier. In Berlin, Jack was greeted by a swarm of women who attempted to rip his clothes off. The management at the Adlon Hotel in Germany swore that they would never again allow Jack to stay at their establishment. They were upset because the hotel detectives spent an inordinate amount of time protecting Jack from overly adoring female fans.

According to Kearns, he informed Tex Rickard that he wanted a "big money bout" and that a Dempsey-Wills fight might be an option. Rickard agreed with Kearns' sentiment. But one thing stood in the way. Rickard told Kearns that "the word came to me right straight from the governor's mansion that we can't fight Wills. They keep remembering all the trouble when Johnson was the champion, and they're afraid of race riots and everything else. We can't fight him simply because he's a Negro. Sounds silly but that's the way they want it."

Undeterred, Kearns contacted Floyd Fitzsimmons and informed him about his desire for a Dempsey-Wills bout. He further informed Fitzsimmons that he didn't care where in the Midwest the bout would be held. Fitzsimmons contacted Kearns and told him how impossible it would be to stage a fight involving the champion and a black contender. "It's no good, Doc," Fitzsimmons warned him. "There just are too many outside influences at work against us." Realizing that a Dempsey-Wills could never occur in the present climate of racial tensions in America, Kearns gave up on his quest.

Dempsey returned to America thoroughly exhausted and almost entirely broke. He wanted another big fight as soon as possible. Jack had heard that Harry Wills was eager to fight him. He wanted to face Wills in the ring, but he soon discovered that the boxing establishment was against the idea. Dempsey was told that the racist boxing establishment didn't want to endure another black heavyweight champion.

Paddy Mullins, Harry Wills' manager, continued to pressure Dempsey into fighting his man. Mullins complained to the New York State Boxing Commission about Dempsey's apparent outright refusal to fight Wills. Unfortunately, Dempsey had no say in the matter. Rickard and Kearns agreed to compromise and promptly drew up a contract on July 11. The contract indicated that a fight between the two boxers would be "set within 60 days after a reliable promoter undertook to stage the bout." Dempsey was warned by the Boxing Commission that he might face suspension if he didn't face Wills in the ring in the near future. No promoter, however, wanted to have anything to do with the bout.

Early in 1923, Kearns considered yet again a rematch with Jess Willard. Tommy Gibbons was another possible contender, but he lacked big name recognition. He was a supreme boxer but he failed to set the world on fire. Kearns publicly announced that he still wanted a Dempsey-Wills match even though privately he knew the chances of such a bout were nil. He announced that the "Wills match is what the public wants most of all and Dempsey is ready to sign for any reasonable terms. I have no bona fide offer for a match with Wills but I am going to insist that it be given first consideration." Apparently, Kearns was trying to appease the New York Boxing Commission so that they would climb off Dempsey's back.

Kearns was determined to promote Jack's future fights. He was supremely confident he could be just as successful as Rickard. He was approached by a group of businessmen from Shelby, Montana. They promised to pay Dempsey and Kearns an enormous sum of money if he agreed to stage the fight in Shelby. Rickard thought it was laughable to stage a fight in a town no one ever heard of. He repeatedly warned Kearns that he was making a big mistake, but Kearns had already made up his mind. Even Dempsey groaned at the idea of fighting in Shelby. Jack gave in to Kearns' promises of a huge payday.

In the meantime, Kearns made arrangements to ensure that a Dempsey-Gibbons fight would indeed take place in the hole-in-the-wall town called Shelby. Kearns was determined more than ever to be the sole promoter of the fight. He refused to listen to Rickard's warnings about Dempsey fighting too often because it might hurt the gate.

According to Dempsey, Tommy Gibbons was a highly

underrated fighter. Dempsey had heard that Gibbons was confident he could beat Jack. All he had to do, he thought, was to avoid Dempsey's punches by displaying some very clever boxing. Gibbons relied on the idea that Jack might be rusty due to his long layoff. After all, Dempsey hadn't had a real fight for years because he was such a devastating puncher. Gibbons was unaware just how vulnerable Dempsey actually was. Reportedly, Jack was nearly knocked out twice while training in Great Falls.

"Gentleman" James J. Corbett thought highly of Tommy Gibbons' boxing skills. "No heavyweight of any era — and that included Dempsey himself — has accomplished anything within a mile of Gibbons' knockout record," Corbett wrote in a syndicated boxing column. "Tommy has ducked no one," Corbett went on to write. "He has gone out of his way to get fights. And all except Bartley Madden were knocked out."

Dempsey had a great deal of respect for Tex Rickard. He believed that Rickard was an honest businessman who looked out for Jack's interests as well as his own. Dempsey was also saddened to hear about Rickard's perilous personal life. Rickard had been accused of luring pre-teenage girls into the back seat of a taxi where he allegedly molested them. The girls accused him of forcing iodine down their throats. Rickard was brought in for questioning by the police. He was subsequently placed in the custody of his attorney. The bail was set at $10,000.

Several other girls came forward and accused Rickard of molesting them. Rickard denied all wrong doing and a trial was scheduled to hear both sides. If Rickard was found guilty of second-degree rape, he could be imprisoned for many years. Rickard was able to prove that he was with a group of friends at a sporting event during the time the alleged molestation and rape took place. The jury returned a not guilty verdict.

A committee of businessmen from Shelby and Mayor Johnson officially agreed to hold a heavyweight title fight in their town. Not only would a heavyweight title fight be good for business, but the fight would finally put Shelby on the map. Tommy Gibbons was so excited about the prospect of fighting Dempsey for the title, he reportedly was willing to fight for nothing.

The committee advised Mike Collins, Gibbons' manager, to reach out to Kearns and offer him $300,000. "Doc" Kearns wired Collins back immediately. He demanded payment of $100,000 immediately, $100,000 a month after the first installment, and $100,000 just before the fight.

As soon as Kearns and Dempsey received the first payment, they traveled to Great Falls, Montana and set up a training camp. Kearns learned that Mayor Johnson was not able to raise the second installment. Kearns was furious. "You've got to pay Dempsey every red cent or you won't see him at all," Kearns threatened. "Don't take us for fools, I warn you!" The committee finally sent another $100,000 as promised. Kearns still felt uneasy about the deal and fumed about it at camp.

When Kearns didn't receive the final installment, he lost his temper and threatened to cancel the bout. Twenty angry citizens traveled all the way from Butte, Montana to speak with "Doc" Kearns. They warned Kearns and Dempsey that they would tar and feather them if the fight didn't go on as planned. Dempsey convinced Kearns that the final $100,000 payment should come out of the gate receipts. Shelby's businessmen could not even afford to pay for the newly built arena. To smooth things over, the lumberman in charge of building the arena was made President of the Dempsey-Gibbons fight.

Dempsey trained at a former beer garden in Great Falls Park, Montana. Jack didn't look very impressive at his sparring sessions. A couple of top graded heavyweights gave Dempsey a hard time in the ring. One of Jack's sparring partners, Jack Burke, knocked Dempsey to the canvas not once, but twice. Dempsey's reflexes were slower than they had ever been and he lumbered across the ring toward his opponent instead of attacking. Many onlookers believed that two years of rust had slowed the once ferocious tiger.

Just days before the fight, Dempsey sparred with British welterweight, Billy Wells. At this point, Dempsey was focusing his attention on improving his speed in the ring. He knew Gibbons was an excellent boxer who moved quickly around the ring. Jack knew that in order to land punches he needed to catch and corner Gibbons. Gibbons was a master at slipping and side-stepping punches and Jack needed to neutralize those defensive tactics.

The fight took place on July 4, 1923. Only 7,202 fans paid to witness the fight. Remarkably, about 4,000 fans slipped into the arena for free. The temperature at fight time was an unbearable 95 degrees. Dempsey stepped into the ring at approximately 3:36 pm to a chorus of boos and jeers. He appeared not to be affected by the crowd's reaction. His long black hair was slicked back and his skin was the color of leather. He looked supremely confident as he stood in his corner, scowling at no one in particular.

Tommy Gibbons entered the ring several minutes later and was greeted with loud cheers and well-wishes. His skin was pale and he looked just as mean and determined as Dempsey. The odds were 2 to 1 in favor of Dempsey.

The ring announcer stood in the middle of the ring and shouted through a megaphone, "Ladies and gentlemen, I take the pleasure in introducing Tommy Gibbons, the contender for the title of the heavyweight championship of the world." A moment later he introduced Dempsey. "I have the pleasure of introducing the Manassa Mauler, Jack Dempsey, heavyweight champion of the world."

It appeared most of the crowd heartily supported Gibbons. Heywood Broun wrote the following: "The unruly crowd wanted Gibbons to win because he is pleasant and agreeable, a good churchman and the father of three charming children. When he became an honorary member of the Blackfeet tribe the other day, the Indians prayed to Mother Earth to make Thunder Chief (Gibbons) as powerful as lightening."

Dempsey rushed toward Gibbons at the opening bell. Dempsey quickly landed some body blows and Gibbons wisely fell into a clinch. Gibbons landed a right to Dempsey's head and Jack responded with a right to Gibbons' face. The challenger recalled that the blow "felt like being slugged with a brick." During the clinches, of which there were many, Dempsey inflicted a lot of damage to the back of Gibbons' neck with rabbit punches. Unfortunately for Gibbons in particular, rabbit punches and kidney punches were allowed in this fight. Kearns had made sure that his fighter was given as much leeway as possible in order to destroy Gibbons.

In the second round, Gibbons landed a hard left to Dempsey's eye. The blow was hard enough to cause a nasty cut over Jack's eye. In between rounds, Kearns applied powder over the injury in a desperate attempt to stop blood from flowing over the eye. A wound such as this could cause a fighter to lose a close match. To make matters worse, some of the powder was inadvertently smeared into Dempsey's eyes. Jack fought partially blind for the next several rounds. Dempsey stalked the challenger and landed blows to the head and body as Gibbons either clinched or sidestepped Dempsey's punches. Gibbons proved that not only could he skillfully neutralize many of Jack's blows, but he could box quite effectively. He never allowed Dempsey to trap him in a corner.

In the third round, Gibbons decided to throw more punches. Rather than clinch or retreat, he stalled Dempsey's attack time and time again with sharp, powerful and effective right and left jabs. Gibbons recalled later: "I kept on the move and forced him to wade through a cross-fire of jabs, hooks and right crosses." Gibbons displayed impressive boxing skills which hampered Dempsey's attack. Near the end of the round, Jack landed a hard blow on the challenger's left side. Dempsey continued his assault with hard blows to Gibbons' head. The challenger was lucky to have survived the round.

The next several rounds followed basically the same pattern. Dempsey relentlessly stalked his prey as Gibbons retreated, blocked punches, clinched or counterpunched. It became very obvious at this point of the fight that Dempsey was vulnerable against a very cagey boxer like Gibbons.

Before the start of the twelfth round, Kearns reminded

Jack that now was the time to put Gibbons away. No one had ever survived a twelfth round against Dempsey. The last fighter to have lasted that long in the ring against Jack was Bill Brennan in 1920. Unlike the Gibbons fight, Dempsey had been way behind in points against Brennan leading into the twelfth.

Dempsey charged Gibbons just as the bell sounded for the start of the round. "In the clinches he mauled me," Gibbons recalled, "jolting me with clubbing rights to the head. I was very tired and his rushes were getting harder to stop." Dempsey landed solid blows to the challenger's head and mid-section. Gibbons grabbed Dempsey's arms in order to stave off more punishment.

The bell for the final round sounded and Dempsey immediately went on the attack. Gibbons feared the worst as he desperately clung onto Dempsey, hoping to survive more punishing short range blows to the midsection. Gibbons must have known that Dempsey was not satisfied with merely winning by a decision. Only a knockout would satisfy the Manassa Mauler. Dempsey frequently missed his target by a wide margin in an attempt to put Gibbons away for good.

Jack was declared the winner after fifteen grueling rounds of boxing. Dempsey was glad the fight lasted fifteen rounds because it helped him get in shape. He firmly believed that going fifteen rounds with Gibbons prevented Firpo from knocking him out in his next title fight.

Dempsey's battle with Tommy Gibbons was, on the surface at least, a lackluster fight. Gibbons displayed some very impressive boxing skills. He had to perform exceedingly well otherwise he would have been annihilated by

Dempsey. The fight crowd, however, had come to witness another Dempsey slaughter, not an exercise on how to box cleverly against a wild panther who liked to end his fights early. The fight also proved that Dempsey had more difficulty coping with good boxers than he had with big, powerful fighters. His battles with Gene Tunney would confirm this notion.

Amazingly, Gibbons was in fairly decent shape after all the punishment he absorbed. Although his lips were cut and his midsection was covered with red welts, he looked to be in fine shape. Gibbons later claimed he could not wear a hat for quite a while due to several large bumps on his head.

Kearns was scorned by everyone in Shelby after the fight. He was blamed by the business community for Shelby going bankrupt. Kearns couldn't have cared less. Many sportswriters were highly critical toward the fight. Gibbons was blasted for refusing to get in close to Dempsey in order to exchange blows. Of course, that would have spelled certain defeat for the challenger. Not everyone agreed with the popular notion that the bout was a snoozer. Damon Runyon referred to the fight as "one of the greatest battles of recent years in the prize ring. Gibbons was the coyote," he wrote, "one of the wisest, fastest and shiftiest animals of the plains, on which this game was played; Dempsey, the greyhound, strong, speedy, alert, dangerous. Running, twisting, doubling, Gibbons, the coyote, got safely home to cover at the end of the long chase, panting a little, bleeding a little — but safe."

Many respectable boxing experts and veteran sportswriters were shocked that Dempsey was not able to put

Gibbons away early in the fight. Rickard was certain the fight wouldn't last more than six rounds. Heywood Broun was certain Gibbons would fall inside two rounds. "The crowd was intensely partisan," Broun wrote, "and Dempsey could not hit his opponent a foot above the belt without cries of 'foul' ringing out. On the other hand, Gibbons could not be criticized for holding on. It is a triumph to last against the champion, Dempsey's short punches to the body carried no such snap as they did against Carpentier. At the moment, he is not the killing Dempsey the ring once knew. The crowd had sobered him. He may yet be dethroned while playing it safe and Luis Firpo might do it."

Grantland Rice was impressed with Gibbons' ability to hurt Dempsey. "After taking a terrible inside hammering in the seventh round," Rice wrote, "he suddenly braced and slugged Dempsey with a whistling right upon the mouth. The force of the blow drove Dempsey's upper lip between his teeth. It was a lusty crack, a free untrammeled blow, and for ten seconds Dempsey worked to get the bruised flesh free."

Damon Runyon was duly impressed with Gibbons' supreme boxing techniques. "He never made a mistake from a boxing standpoint," Runyon observed. "He could never have won fighting as he did; he never will win an important battle fighting as he did." Runyon, however, was in awe of Gibbons' survival instincts against a killing machine like Jack Dempsey.

"We took in $132,000 at the gate," Kearns explained, "and that, with the $200,000 I had, saw Jack and me through. Jack and I were not very popular. Jack got away on one of the night specials, but I had to wait an hour or so to clear things up. Eventually I paid five hundred bucks for a special engine to take me to Great Falls."

Tommy Gibbons was paid $50,000 by the motion pictures. He also obtained a theatrical booking. When asked why he fought for a living, he replied that he had to fight to eat. "I have a big family and I have to support them," he explained. "I fought Dempsey on a percentage basis and he got just about every penny that made its way through the gate. Sure, I took a chance — and lost. What little money I had was deposited in the bank in Shelby, which went bust. What a mess. I did, however, get a vaudeville contract. I had to compete with trained seals to get enough money to feed the wife and kids."

Gibbons and his family were well received when they stepped off the train in his hometown of St. Paul, Minnesota. Appreciative hometown fans showered their hero with flowers. Tommy Gibbons, after all, was one of the very few fighters to face Jack Dempsey and not end up being counted out. Even more impressive was the fact that he lasted the entire fight without having been mauled to death.

Dempsey went back to Hollywood for fun, relaxation, and investments. Kearns and Dempsey began investing in Los Angeles real estate property. Jack bought a beautiful house on Western Avenue in Hollywood. He spared no expense. He even had his walls and floors covered with expensive Persian rugs. Jack invited his mother to live with him. She obliged but soon grew homesick. She had divorced her husband and was used to living alone in Salt Lake City.

Rickard, always on the lookout for fresh and intriguing talent, was fascinated with Luis Angel Firpo's strength and endurance. He hired Jimmy De Forest to train Firpo for a possible match with Dempsey. The Argentinian stood six feet three inches tall and weighed about 225 pounds.

Rickard announced to the boxing world that Luis Firpo would soon face Jess Willard. The winner of that fight would go on to challenge Dempsey for the title. Yankee Stadium was chosen as the site for the bout. New York commissioner William Muldoon determined that Jess Willard was too old to fight and was therefore banned from fighting in the Empire State. Rickard promptly announced that the fight would instead take place at Boyle's Thirty Acres in Jersey City, New Jersey.

According to sportswriter Hype Igoe, Tex Rickard was an astute judge of boxers. "I never knew a man who was quicker to sense a great match," he wrote in *Ring* magazine, "to foresee the dramatic possibilities of a proposed bout than Tex Rickard. I happened to be in Tex's office the day that Luis Firpo entered and Tex laid eyes on the Argentine. Luis had just collected $125 for a fight in Jersey City with Sailor Maxted. He had knocked Maxted kicking like a sea crab and Tex had sent for Luis. It was that sense of the dramatic that had appealed to Tex, the big fellow possessing a wallop. Firpo had sold himself as soon as Tex laid his peepers on him. Tex's cold, discerning eyes were drinking in Firpo's shaggy frame like rare wine. I saw Tex mentally whip a tape measure all over Firpo. When Luis left, up spoke Tex. 'God, what a man! Hype, he and Dempsey will make the greatest fight you ever seed.' He slapped me on the back and laughed. I never saw Tex so happy as then. That was picking them. That was knowing fighters and fights."

Firpo's trainer, Jimmy De Forest, was the first to admit that his fighter was slow, even awkward, and lacked good defensive skills. Firpo may have sensed that himself because he was such a powerful puncher who didn't feel the need to learn even basic defensive tactics. Reporters who witnessed Firpo's sparring sessions were impressed with the fighter's newfound boxing skills.

De Forest paid the 45-year old former heavyweight champion, Jack Johnson, $250 to spar with the Argentinian. Johnson played to the crowd as he occasionally made the clumsy Firpo appear foolish. He easily sidestepped many of Firpo's wild punches. He taunted his victim by holding and squeezing Firpo's arms, thus neutralizing the Argentinian's ability to land blows. Some spectators must have wondered if perhaps Jack Johnson should become a legitimate contender for the heavyweight crown.

On March 12, 1923, Bill Brennan faced Luis Angel Firpo at Madison Square Garden. The bout was scheduled for fifteen rounds but many boxing experts thought the fight would end much sooner. A small crowd of about 12,000 paid approximately $50,755 to witness the event. Firpo tipped the scales at 220 pounds while Brennan weighed in at 203 pounds.

Both fighters gave it their all throughout the fight. Firpo and Brennan hammered away at each other like wild beasts in a do or die battle to the death. Brennan landed several left jabs at Firpo's face. One of those jabs opened up a cut over Firpo's left eye. In round six, Firpo failed to land several wild punches as Brennan slipped and side-stepped most of them. In the twelfth round, however, Firpo bored in toward his adversary and let loose a barrage of lefts and rights. Brennan dropped to the canvas and stayed there even after the bell rang. The crowd erupted with cheers for the Argentinian. Shockingly, it was revealed after the bout that referee Jack Appell had almost ended the fight in favor of Brennan due to the nasty cut over Firpo's eye. So much blood flowed from Firpo's wound that Appell believed the Argentinian was seriously injured. He was reportedly pressured by Jimmy De Forest and Chairman William Muldoon not to end the fight.

Brennan announced that the better man won the contest. He thought Firpo was a natural fighter who didn't necessarily need to understand the science of boxing because he was so strong and powerful. Sadly, Brennan lay unconscious in a hospital for several hours. He had suffered a concussion of the brain. Brennan foolishly refused to end his career as a boxer. Several months later he faced Billy Miske in Omaha. He was promptly knocked out in the fourth round.

On July 12, 1923, former heavyweight champion Jess Willard took on Luis Firpo at Boyles Thirty Acres in Jersey City, New Jersey. The fight was called the "Battle of the Giants." Firpo was a 5 to 3 favorite going into the fight. On the day of the fight Willard weighed 242 pounds to Firpo's 214 pounds. The Argentinian stood at six feet, two and a half inches, several inches shorter than the towering ex-heavyweight champion.

Firpo took the advice of his trainer, Jimmy De Forest, and concentrated his main assault on Willard's midsection. In the first round, Firpo charged at Willard with a vengeance. Firpo backed Willard into the ropes and landed a barrage of blows. Willard was able to block many of Firpo's punches, however.

In round two, Willard managed to block and slip

Firpo's hard rights and left hooks. Willard's left side was a mass of red welts, more evidence of just how hard Firpo could punch. For the next several rounds, Willard fought a defensive fight. He sensed that it was virtually impossible for him to put Firpo away. His only recourse was to survive Firpo's brutal assaults and perhaps land a lucky haymaker to Firpo's jaw, thus ending the fight.

By the eighth round, Willard was thoroughly exhausted and hurt from Firpo's ferocious barrage of blows to the stomach and kidneys. Willard lowered his hands to protect his battered midsection and Firpo landed several hard blows to his opponent's head. Unable to withstand any more punishment, Willard dropped to one knee. He stayed in that position as he held on to the ropes to steady himself. He was mercifully counted out by referee Harry Lewis.

Reportedly, the fight attracted about 76,000 spectators and grossed approximately $493,000. Willard took home around $123,000 and Firpo pocketed approximately $79,000. The Willard-Firpo fight had the distinction of drawing the biggest crowd ever for a non-championship boxing match.

Kearns was ecstatic about the prospect of Dempsey facing Firpo in the ring. "We'll take him if he'll fight us," Kearns bragged to reporters. "But we're gonna need a million dollars up front. You only get crowds like this because Dempsey had gotten everybody excited about boxing. Look at all the publicity we got for boxing way the hell out there in Shelby. We gotta have a million bucks."

Surprisingly, Firpo was initially dead set against facing Dempsey in the ring. Rickard set him straight by warning him that he must fight Dempsey soon or forget about ever fighting him. Rickard explained that Dempsey and Firpo were in excellent condition and the public would pay a great deal of money to see them battle it out.

Rickard and Kearns were now on speaking terms. Both of them agreed that Rickard should promote the Dempsey-Firpo fight. Kearns was obviously way over his head when it came to promoting fights, even with a fighter of Dempsey's caliber. Rickard arranged a $500,000 guarantee for Dempsey. Kearns badly needed the money. He even owed Dempsey $150,000.

Rickard began promoting the challenger as the "Wild Bull of the Pampas." The name caught on with the public and the press. Dempsey hadn't heard much about Firpo except that he had defeated a number of boxers in South America. Jack initially thought that Firpo was just some "big, clumsy ox." Rickard tried to convince Dempsey that Firpo was a good fighter who possessed a solid right hand punch that could do a tremendous amount of damage. Jack was unimpressed.

Luis Firpo had gained a lot of respect over the years. There were those who questioned Dempsey's chances of stopping the Argentinian in his tracks. Firpo was simply too powerful and dangerous. Joe McCabb, a highly-rated sparring partner, proclaimed, "I've seen Dempsey fight. I know from experience how Firpo fights. I don't think anyone, that, including Dempsey, can hit Firpo hard enough to stop him."

Firpo trained at a dog track in Atlantic City, New Jersey. The track was the same site where Dempsey had trained for his fight against Georges Carpentier. Firpo did not get along at all with the press. He hated interviews and insulted everyone around him. One of the few things he did like was eating. Reporters were shocked to see him swallow huge portions of food and then nonchalantly drop off to sleep.

Many of those who had witnessed Firpo in action were not very impressed with his fighting ability. His critics thought he was extremely powerful but clumsy. He could obviously punch, but could he withstand a Dempsey onslaught? Rickard warned his distractors not to be too judgmental about the Argentinian.

Jack Kearns knew very little about Luis Firpo's abilities in the ring. In order to learn more about the challenger, Kearns sent two of his men to Firpo's training camp. They informed Kearns that Firpo was unusually strong and he punched with extraordinary power. He didn't rely on boxing at all. Instead, he relentlessly plowed forward toward his opponent. Witnesses warned Kearns that he could "take you out" with a single blow.

Many sportswriters criticized Firpo for his apparent lack of boxing skills. He was regarded by many as clumsy and brutish. Dempsey, however, slowly began to respect Firpo's ability to beat top heavyweight contenders. Dempsey listened intently to stories about the Argentinian's impressive knockout record. "Firpo had a terrific right-hand blow," Jack recalled "that could stun a bull, but most observers believed it could be avoided easily. I took descriptions of Firpo's clumsiness with many grains of salt. In this country, he had beaten, in rapid succession and with apparent ease, Bill Brennan, Jack McAuliffe, and Jess Willard. Anyone who could do that was certainly formidable. No one who was as awkward as they said Firpo was could have put away Bill Brennan."

According to Kearns, he thought Firpo would have a difficult time landing a punch against a bobbing and weaving Dempsey. Kearns further reasoned that Jack could easily box Firpo until he saw an opening and then unleash a barrage of blows to end the fight. Kearns was concerned, however, that the fans might be bored with such a tactic. More importantly, he wanted good press and so he decided that the champion should out-slug the challenger until one of them dropped, preferably the challenger.

Tex Rickard claimed, at least publicly, that he thought Dempsey might have a difficult time defeating Firpo. "Take it easy, boys," Rickard advised reporters. "Watch what you say. You may have to eat those words. When the time is right, and I put Firpo in the same ring as Dempsey, why, the public's goin' to be so anxious they'll be willing to put a mortgage on the old homestead just to buy a ticket."

The famous oil tycoon, J. Paul Getty, paid Dempsey a visit at his training camp. He was an avid boxing fan. He even had an expensive gymnasium built inside the basement of his luxurious mansion. Dempsey sparred with Getty in the ring. The tycoon proved to be quite a boxer. He was extremely fast on his feet. Impressed by his own boxing skills, Getty pleaded with Dempsey to fight back harder.

"Go ahead," he yelled to Dempsey, "I can take it."

Within seconds, Getty was sprawled out on the canvas, writhing in pain. His brash manner disappeared and he returned back to his oil fields.

The Dempsey-Firpo fight took place on September 14, 1923, at the Polo Grounds in New York. Mounted policemen were busy controlling a boisterous crowd of raucous boxing fans. As with the Carpentier fight, well-heeled spectators sitting at ringside reflected a virtual Who's Who of famous dignitaries and celebrates from all corners of the world. Tex Rickard was excited about the prospect of having promoted yet another million-dollar gate bout.

"We got another million-dollar gate!" he proudly yelled at Dempsey. "If you put him away with the first punch," he warned Jack, "all those people out there won't get their money's worth." Dempsey observed that unlike Carpentier, Firpo was a very dangerous fighter who could punch hard and take a punch as well. He was big and strong and vicious. Jack had proved he could more than hold his own against big, powerful punchers. Firpo, however, seemed to be in a class by himself.

"Listen, Tex," Dempsey warned Rickard. "There's one difference between this guy and Carpentier. He is bigger and a slugger. He could kill me with one wallop."

Rickard tried to convince Dempsey that Firpo was not as formidable as Jack imagined.

"He's slow and moves like an old tub," Rickard claimed. "I hate to think of all them nice millionaires going out of here sore at both of us."

Rickard's audacity infuriated Dempsey.

"Go to hell!" Dempsey screamed.

Shortly before the historic battle between Dempsey and Firpo, the champion spoke with Grantland Rice about his career thus far.

"I have had to come up through a very hard school where I was fighting not to win but for my existence. I think that's why in the early days I could come back after being knocked down three or four times. Gunboat Smith hit me squarely on the chin with so much force that all I remember is starting to fall forward. I felt my knees giving way and that is about all I remember. Some instinct from the hard, early days kept me going and I won. I don't remember that. I know I won only because they told me."

Dempsey became philosophical about what kind of a fighter he currently was. He understood that he was no longer the desperate, hungry hobo willing to fight just to eat.

"Maybe I can't take as much now as I took then. It's much easier you know and more fun fighting your way up the hill than it is standing on the top and defending it. Being champion isn't as great as it seemed before I was champion. I have more money and softer living, but there are more worries and troubles and cares than I ever dreamed of before. The glory and even the money don't mean as much as they did in the days when you belonged only to your self — not to the public."

Rice asked Dempsey how long he expected to reign supreme over all heavyweight contenders. Jack replied that there was no way of determining that.

"But I know this," Dempsey explained. "When I hit the floor and I can't get up, it will be because a better man put me there. I promise this. After I been down for ten with someone standing over me, I'll never alibi."

Sitting at ringside were such notables as Florenz Ziegfeld, New York Giants manager John J. McGraw, and baseball's greatest slugger, Babe Ruth. Also attending the fight was none other than the infamous mob leader Lucky Luciano. Luciano had reportedly purchased 200 ring side seat tickets for the fight. He could well afford the $2,500. According to Jonathan Van Meter, author of *The Last Good Time*, Luciano made it known to dignitaries and celebrities that he was giving away very expensive, hard to get tickets. Apparently, the New York mobster was attempting to improve his tarnished image as a drug-dealing criminal. Reportedly, Florenz Ziegfeld, Bernard Gimbel, from the famous Gimbel Brothers stores, Al Capone, and many other newsworthy characters from all walks of life took him up on his gracious offer.

Firpo entered the ring first. He wore a dressing gown filled with yellow and black checkers. Moments later the champion entered the ring to thunderous applause. Evidently the slacker charges leveled against him had diminished over time. He wore the customary white boxing trunks and a hooded white sweater. Long gone was the old, tattered woolen sweater he had worn in previous battles. Dempsey weighed 192 pounds, the heaviest he had ever weighed. Not to be outdone, Firpo weighed an impressive 216 pounds.

Joe Humphreys stood in the center of the ring and announced to the crowd: "In this corner, one of the greatest of all heavyweight champions at 192 and a half pounds, Jack Dempsey. And in this corner, the challenger from Argentina, the pride of all South America, at 216 and a half pounds, Luis Angel Firpo." The champion was a 3 to 1 favorite.

In the first round, Dempsey charged Firpo with both fists. Dempsey threw a jab, pounded the challenger with a left and then missed with his right. Just as Dempsey leaned back, Firpo smashed him with a right-hand square on his cheekbone. Jack dropped to one knee from the blow. It marked the first time Jack had touched the canvas since his loss to Fireman Jim Flynn in 1917. Already the fight had become memorable. Sensing an upset, the crowd rose to its feet and screamed hysterically. Dempsey recalled later that had he not been moving away from Firpo at the moment Firpo hit him, he would have been knocked out cold.

Suddenly realizing how dangerous Firpo actually was, Dempsey immediately went on the attack. He instinctively pounded Firpo's body with lethal left hooks and hard rights. Dempsey did what no man had ever done before. He knocked Firpo down. He proceeded to knock Firpo down several more times in the round. Jack nonchalantly stepped over Firpo's body as the Argentinian lay on the canvas in agony. As the challenger attempted to rise, Jack hit him with devastating blows to the head. Kearns yelled, "Jesus! What's holding this guy up?"

Firpo charged Dempsey with blistering lefts and rights, backing him against the ropes. Firpo shot an overhead right at Dempsey's head and Jack fell through the ropes and landed head first on top of several surprised spectators. Dempsey, by now dazed and confused, climbed back into the ring. Firpo immediately tried to finish off the champion with a barrage of wild rights and lefts.

Firpo moved in for the kill. Jack bobbed and weaved to avoid being knocked out. Dempsey went into a clinch in order to ride out the storm. The bell finally sounded, ending perhaps the most exciting first round in heavyweight boxing history. Firpo failed to put Dempsey away largely because of Jack's ability to survive a vicious beating.

At the end of the round, Dempsey walked back to his corner and rested while Kearns and the rest of Jack's corner men argued. They frantically tried to find smelling salts because Jack was still dizzy from the fall. Kearns finally pulled a bottle of smelling salts out of his shirt pocket and shoved it under Jack's nose. The corner men took turns slapping Jack's face in order to snap him out of his stupor.

Much has been written about Dempsey falling through the ropes and landing on the laps of spectators sitting at ringside. One argument claims that Dempsey would never have survived Firpo's attack had he not been shoved out of the ring. By falling out of the ring, Dempsey actually escaped certain defeat. According to this argument, Dempsey was actually "saved" because he was on the verge of being knocked out by the Argentinian. The fight film reveals quite plainly that Dempsey was ultimately shoved through the ropes by Firpo, not punched out of the ring. At the time, Firpo had been throwing wild lefts and rights at Dempsey's head and Jack appeared to be caught off guard by the sudden barrage of fists coming at him from all directions. When Jack finally did get back in the ring, he was able to evade many of Firpo's blows by simply clinching.

Dempsey recounted later that "Exactly what happened during the battle is, in my own personal recollection, exceedingly uncertain. A heavy blow on the head has sometimes the peculiar effect of not only destroying your memory of whatever happened directly afterward, but also of destroying the memory of what happened immediately *before*."

Incredibly, Dempsey asked his corner what round he was knocked out in.

"You just slipped," Kearns explained. "You're coming out for the second. Go out there and box this guy carefully. Let him think you're still groggy and look for the right opening."

Dempsey was relieved to hear that he had miraculously survived the round. He was able to think clearly thanks to his quick recuperative powers He claimed later that he "fought in a complete haze, defensively. I hit, as I remember it," Jack recalled, "not so much to knock him out as to defend myself. The ring seemed to me to be full of Firpos and the air full of boxing gloves. His shaggy hair made him seem like some terrible caveman or gorilla. Certainly, I have never, before or since, fought a man who could deliver so many powerful blows in so short a time. There was no science about it; there was just incredible speed and power. There was also his incredible vitality. Each time he went down, he bounced back to his feet, and the fight went on."

Jack approached Firpo a lot more cautiously in the second round. He now respected Firpo's punching power and resilience. This time he would be careful not to get hit by the Wild Bull. Dempsey went on the offensive. He threw devastating punches at Firpo's head and midsection. Firpo dropped to the canvas in excruciating pain. Dempsey stood close to the challenger as the referee counted over the fallen Firpo. Dempsey landed more blows to Firpo's mid-section and the Argentinian dropped to the canvas again. Firpo was finally counted out. Dempsey rushed over to the stricken challenger, lifted him to his feet and then helped him walk back to his corner.

"That Rickard wanted a good fight," Kearns shouted. "Well, we gave him one. Maybe the greatest one of all."

Dempsey was amazed how many people took credit for breaking his fall in the infamous first round and then claimed to have pushed him back into the ring. Several people, including Walter Winchell, George Bellows, and Milton Berle asserted that they played a key part in helping Jack in one way or another.

The fight created a lot of controversy. Bill Muldoon, chairman of the New York Boxing Commission, interrogated "Kid" McPartland concerning his role with assisting Dempsey back into the ring.

"What were you doing, trying to help Dempsey?" Muldoon grilled McPartland.

"What would you do, Commissioner," McPartland replied, "if somebody threw a medicine ball at you? You'd put up your hands, wouldn't you?"

Muldoon, satisfied with McPartland's reasonable response, ended the interview.

Grantland Rice reported that he had just witnessed "the most sensational fighting ever seen in any ring back through all the ages of the ancient game." Heywood Broun of the *World* was equally impressed with the spectacle. "It is not possible," he wrote, "that there has ever before been such a battle for the heavyweight championship."

Jack grasped only too well the notion that he had narrowly escaped almost certain defeat after having been knocked out of the ring. He firmly believed that he would have easily beaten Firpo in a rubber match. But his fight with Firpo made Jack realize that he was no longer the fighter he once was when he took the heavyweight title away from Jess Willard in 1919.

Firpo was paid an impressive $156,250 for his performance in the ring. He complained vehemently that he had really won the fight. "I won it four times on fouls and bad refereeing. Once when Dempsey hit me low. Two times when he hit me while I was getting up. And once after I knocked him out of the ring. The rules said you had to get back without help. I saw what happened. So many American writers pushed Dempsey into the ring that it looked like he was getting a back massage."

Dempsey was harshly criticized by the media regarding the size of his purse. In comparison, super slugger Babe Ruth earned $50,000 that same year. The *Christian Science Monitor* came down particularly hard on Jack. The newspaper questioned whether it was morally permissible for Dempsey to have been so well paid for a boxing match when servicemen faced death in the trenches during the Great War, only to return to their homeland to barely eke out a living.

Shortly after the slugfest, Dempsey told Firpo how sorry he was for hitting him as soon as he got back on his feet from a knockdown. He explained to the Argentinian that he was dazed and confused at the time when he pounded Firpo to the canvas. "There were three of us in the ring, Jack," Firpo responded rather wryly, "so if you didn't know what you were doing, why didn't you hit the referee?"

Grantland Rice firmly believed that Dempsey should have lost the title to Firpo. According to Rice, Dempsey punched the challenger immediately after a clinch instead of stepping away. Dempsey allegedly walloped Firpo right after the bell sounded ending the first round. Rice wrote that both incidents were definitely "actions for which he might have been disqualified then and there." Rice, however, cut Dempsey some slack for possibly being "so badly hurt by Firpo's terrific wallops that he was in a mental daze — completely out of his head."

Nat Fleischer was another highly influential boxing authority who thought the title should have been taken away from Jack. "Firpo should be wearing the crown,"

Fleischer claimed right after Dempsey's stunning victory.

Gene Tunney was very impressed with Dempsey's uncanny ability to take severe punishment and still stalk his victim. "Against Firpo," Tunney acknowledged, "Dempsey showed me something else; that he could take it. I don't believe any other human alive could have absorbed all those full-arm blows from Firpo and remained upright or even conscious, let alone win the fight."

The public by and large had a different take on the fight. They were very impressed with Dempsey's uncanny ability to survive Firpo's brutality and raw savageness and still come out on top. Jack's ability to climb back into the ring and fight off a vicious all-out attack by Firpo stood uppermost in the public's mind. They were willing to forgive Dempsey's shocking indiscretions in the ring.

Dempsey was in agonizing pain after the fight. His backside ached from the fall. Kearns desperately drove crazed fans away from Jack's dressing room. Dempsey was thoroughly exhausted from the fight and understandably wanted to be left alone so he could rest.

The champion was determined to visit Rickard before Kearns could get to him. Jack had grown tired of Kearns always grabbing the winnings first and blowing a huge portion before splitting it with Dempsey. He was fed up with Kearns' selfish attitude. Rickard totally agreed with Dempsey's sentiments and promptly paid him $550,000. Kearns exploded when he discovered that Jack had seemingly gone behind his back.

"What the hell you going to do with that money?" Kearns screamed at Jack.

"Well, I'm putting two hundred thousand in a trust

fund," Jack explained.

"What interest?" Kearns snapped.

Jack told him that he didn't know for sure. Kearns looked at Dempsey like he was trash. Dempsey paid a price for his actions. Kearns tore into Jack for being dishonest.

"You damn fool!" Kearns screamed at Jack. "Why, I could have doubled the dough for you. What the hell's the matter with you? Ain't my advice good enough for you no more?"

Dempsey knew how important it was to put his money away in a trust. He knew one day he would lose the title and he desperately wanted financial security. Jack was convinced that had Firpo been a little more aggressive in the ring, he might have lost the title. It was therefore essential for him to build up some net worth.

A major change in boxing occurred after the controversial Dempsey-Firpo fight. The change would one day play a crucial role in Dempsey's future. The "neutral corner" rule was adopted. The rule stated that once a fighter scored a knockdown, he must immediately go to the farthest neutral corner. The count would not begin until the fighter reached that corner. Dempsey admitted later that he didn't particularly pay heed to the rule. It was a decision he would soon deeply regret.

Because of the controversy surrounding the way Dempsey climbed back into the ring after being shoved out of it, another rule was revised. At the time of the fight, the rule indicated that a fighter had to immediately return to the ring, otherwise the hapless fighter would be declared the loser. The ruling failed to indicate a specific time in which the fighter needed to get back into the ring. The new rule closed this loop hole by specifying a time limit of ten seconds by which a fighter needed to return to the ring after having been knocked out of it.

On September 14, 1923, the *New York Times* printed an article about Luis Firpo. The article indicated that he was "not sore about not winning the Dempsey fight." Instead, Firpo suggested that his handlers didn't protest against fouls Dempsey had apparently committed during the fight. He went on, however, to insist that it would not have made any difference. He claimed that Damon Runyon thought Dempsey really lost the fight, "but that's all over now."

CHAPTER SEVEN

DEMPSEY VS TUNNEY

Gene Tunney and Jack Dempsey pose prior to doing battle in the ring.

Dempsey and Kearns continued to disagree about money and women. "Doc" Kearns didn't want his fighter involved with women at all. In Kearns' opinion, boxing and women needed to be mutually exclusive.

"You don't need dames and all the emotional baggage they carry with them," Kearns warned Dempsey. "Prizefighting and dolls don't mix, so lay off 'em, kid."

Jack had grown weary listening to Kearns' stern tirades about his personal life. He recognized that Kearns was always seeing women and partying at all hours of the night. The double standard was more than Dempsey could bear so he began questioning Kearns about the status of their assets. Kearns became defensive whenever Jack brought up as sensitive a subject as Dempsey's finances. Jack didn't appreciate being kept in the dark. He was extremely concerned about his share of the money and where it was actually going.

Over the next several years Dempsey fought in several exhibition bouts. None of his opponents posed any real threat to Jack. Many of the bouts were scheduled for four rounds. Jack didn't train hard for these exhibitions. Dempsey was usually paid several thousand dollars for each exhibition.

Tex Rickard had difficulty trying to find a qualified opponent for Dempsey. He was interested in promoting a heavyweight title fight that would grab the attention of the public like never before. Several people floated Sam Langford's name as a viable contender. Rickard refused to entertain the idea outright for racial reasons. Reportedly, Dempsey didn't want to face the Boston Bonecrusher because he feared Langford had a reasonable chance of beating him.

One afternoon Jack was strolling down Hollywood Boulevard. He noticed a very attractive woman staring at a billboard. He decided to introduce himself to the lovely lady. He asked her if perhaps he had seen her once before. Realizing she was not impressed with his approach, Jack offered to introduce himself.

"Listen buster," the lady warned him. "Allow me to tell you to scram before I scream for help!"

Alarmed, Jack quickly walked away from the lady. He began to reconsider Kearns' advice about staying away from women. Perhaps his manager was right all along. Finding a woman might not be worth the trouble.

One day Jack Dougherty approached Dempsey and asked him if he would like to meet a Hollywood starlet. Dempsey liked the idea and so Dougherty drove Jack to a location where a motion picture was being shot. The name of the movie was *The Alaskan*. It starred Thomas Meighan and Estelle Taylor. Immediately after they arrived at the movie location, Jack was introduced to the female lead, Estelle Taylor. Jack instantly recognized her and was horrified. The actress was the same woman who had given Jack the brush off. Dempsey was smitten by Estelle's beauty and charm. Now that she had been properly introduced to Jack, Estelle began seeing him quite frequently.

Estelle Taylor had traveled all the way from Wilmington, Delaware to Hollywood in search of fame and fortune. She had won a local beauty contest that allowed her to model for artists. She attended the Sargent School of Dramatic Arts in New York. She landed several small roles in pictures produced by Fox. Eventually, she starred opposite the great John Barrymore in the motion picture, *Don Juan.*

Estelle received a lot of bad publicity over her affair with George Walsh, a married man. Paramount also felt the heat over her involvement with another man. Estelle decided to end her contract with the motion picture studio. She may have heard that she was about to be fired by Walter Wanger, a new producer for Paramount.

Jack felt sorry for Estelle and tried to console her. He bought her a brand-new Buick to replace her old Willys-Overland. Jack began to neglect his career. He was careful not to tell anyone in his inner circle about his relationship with a Hollywood actress. Even Kearns was totally in the dark about Jack's relationship with Estelle. Complicating matters even further was the fact that Estelle had a husband. She was married to Kenneth Peabody, a wholesale furniture store clerk. It seemed all of Hollywood knew about their affair except Kearns and Peabody.

As soon as Dempsey asked Estelle to marry him, she asked her husband for a divorce. At first, Peabody considered suing Dempsey but later changed his mind. He may have assumed that because he had not lived with his wife for several years, the chances of winning in court were nil.

Dempsey decided to introduce Kearns to Estelle. The two of them disliked each other from the very beginning. Estelle didn't think Kearns was looking out for Dempsey's best interests and Kearns thought Estelle was a gold digger, out to take Jack for all his money. Dempsey called Kearns soon after he married Estelle. He wanted to tell Kearns the good news.

"Congratulate me!" Jack yelled to Kearns over the

phone.

"Did what?" Kearns replied. "Speak up. I can't hear you."

"I'm married," Jack repeated.

"What? Who to?"

"Estelle. Hold on, she wants to talk to you."

Furious, Kearns slammed down the receiver.

Kearns and Dempsey didn't see or speak to each other for several weeks. Finally, Kearns asked the Dempseys to meet him at a restaurant, the Montmarte, in Hollywood. Jack and Estelle arrived early and waited nervously for Kearns to make his entrance. Jack's trainer, Teddy Hayes, accompanied the couple. Kearns arrived at the restaurant inebriated and late. He sat down at their table and began spewing insinuations at the top of his lungs. Kearns turned to Estelle and informed her that he had investigated her past and what he discovered wasn't pretty.

Kearns threatened to destroy Estelle if she didn't coop-erate with him. Dempsey was visibly shaken and warned Kearns to lay off his wife. Kearns shrugged off Jack's threat and swigged more liquor from his flask. Unable to stand anymore of Kearns' threats, Estelle quickly rose to her feet and yelled at Kearns for threatening her. She told Kearns that she had plenty of dirt on him that would bury his career. She alluded to an incident involving Kearns that allegedly occurred in Tijuana. Exasperated, Estelle turned to her husband.

"I'm leaving, Jack. Are you staying or coming with me?"

As Jack and Estelle left the Montmarte, Kearns turned to Teddy and told him how he felt about Dempsey.

"Listen, I don't give a damn where the hell I am. I found

him as a bum and I'll make sure he'll go back as a bum."

As soon as they returned home, Estelle told Dempsey to immediately fire Kearns. Jack pleaded with her to calm down. Kearns had been his manager for a long time. He still felt obligated for all that Kearns had done for him. He argued that his boxing career had been going essentially nowhere until Kearns took him under his wing. Unmoved by Dempsey's pleadings, Estelle wanted Jack to make his decision right then and there.

Out of desperation, Dempsey called Kearns to try and smooth things over. Kearns blamed Dempsey for ruining their partnership. Jack accused Kearns of not being totally fair as far as Jack's finances were concerned. Dempsey decided that he could no longer tolerate Kearns as his manager. Their partnership of seven years was now over.

Shortly after Dempsey and Kearns split, Jack had his nose surgically reshaped. Apparently, Estelle had never been satisfied with Dempsey's pug nose. In fact, she had told Louella Parsons, a Hollywood columnist, that she thought Jack had one of the least desirable pugs she had ever seen. Dempsey was only too happy to please his wife.

Teddy Hayes did not approve of Jack's new nose. He thought Dempsey's new appendage might change his style of fighting in the ring. He felt the champion might become overly concerned about protecting his nose in the ring. He even feared Jack might transition into a defensive fighter rather than remain an outstanding aggressive swarmer. Any tinkering with Dempsey's fighting tactics could very well cost him the title.

While Dempsey informed the boxing world that he was in the market for a new manager, Kearns warned anyone who would listen that Dempsey was untrustworthy. According to Kearns, Dempsey was an ingrate whose word was totally worthless. He also accused Tex Rickard of turning Jack against him.

Jack and Estelle traveled to Europe for their honeymoon. They visited Paris, Cologne, and Berlin and were greeted by enthusiastic fans. Dempsey took time out to box in several exhibitions. While in Berlin, he was introduced to a young, up and coming heavyweight, Max Schmeling. Jack was surprised how closely they resembled each other. The two fighters sparred together for a few minutes while Dempsey provided Schmeling with some boxing pointers. Dempsey was impressed with Schmeling's boxing skills and even predicted that one day he could be a heavyweight champion.

Soon after the Dempseys returned to Hollywood they bought a luxurious house on Los Feliz Boulevard. The property included an eighteen-hole golf course and a swimming pool. Estelle spent most of her time reading and entertaining company. One of Estelle's closest friends was Lupe Velez. Velez constantly complained to Estelle that Dempsey was well beneath Estelle's social ranking. Jack grew tired of Velez's insults and warned Estelle not to invite her over anymore. Estelle told Jack that her friend was always welcome. She warned her husband that he should do something about his friends. She didn't like the way they constantly stared at her while they sat around the house like vagrants for hours on end.

Dempsey hired a business manager by the name of Gene Normile. He trusted Normile because he was, according to Jack, financially well off. Estelle didn't want Dempsey to take investment advice from anyone except her. Estelle convinced Jack to invest in one of their movies, *Manhattan Madness*. The movie flopped.

In 1925, the New York State Athletic Commission declared Dempsey ineligible to fight in the state of New York. Their decision was based on the fact that Dempsey refused to fight Harry Wills. Jack was more than willing to fight Wills, but the boxing community, including well established promoters like Tex Rickard, refused to have anything to do with such a match.

According to Dempsey, Kearns actually did attempt to arrange a fight between the two men. The fight was tentatively scheduled to take place on September 24, but no one came forward to promote it. Rickard was almost certain the fight could easily pull in at least a million dollars, but that was not enough for him to get involved with the match-up between a white champion and a black challenger. Ex-heavyweight champion Jack Johnson was still too fresh on many people's minds.

Rickard was much more interested in having Dempsey face a relatively unknown boxer named Gene Tunney. Tunney was rising quickly in the heavyweight division due to his incredible boxing abilities. Tunney was also an ex-Marine and women loved him because of his movie-star looks and charisma.

On many levels, Gene Tunney was the direct opposite of Jack Dempsey. Tunney was a bookworm who enjoyed reading classic literature, such as *The Three Musketeers, The Way of All Flesh,* and *The Rubaiyat.* He considered himself somewhat of a literary critic who primarily read to relax. The fighting styles between Jack Dempsey and Gene Tunney were almost polar opposites. Dempsey relentlessly charged his opponent, trying to create an opening by which he could then unleash a blistering attack. He believed that the best defense was a good offence. Jack tried to end each fight as quickly as possible. Tunney, on the other, was a supreme boxer. He was a terrific counter puncher who didn't concern himself with ending a fight quickly.

According to Tunney, Dempsey's fighting style made him predictable in the ring. All an excellent boxer who could punch had to do was fight Jack from a distance and throw wicked left jabs in order to keep him off balance and lightning fast overhand rights to Dempsey's jaw. This was, of course, easier said than done.

Many sportswriters who interviewed Tunney were put off by his apparent air of smugness. A friend of Tunney's confessed that he indeed "affected a superiority" which he found very annoying. He also claimed that the boxer "used long words when shorter, more easily understood words would have served a clearer purpose." Many others were upset by the fact that Tunney was very particular whom he allowed in his private circle of friends and acquaintances. Tunney appeared to feel more comfortable with the likes of powerful industrialists, artists, writers, and professors.

Gene Tunney was well aware of his image as a fighter. "It has been argued," he once related in an article about his ring prowess, "that I was a synthetic fighter. That was true. They said I lacked the killer instinct, which was also true. I found no joy in knocking people unconscious or battering their faces. The lust for battle and massacre was missing. I had a notion that the killer instinct was really founded in fear, that the killer of the ring raged with ruthless brutality because deep down he was afraid. Synthetic fighter, not a killer! There was a kind of angry resentment in the accusation. People might have reasoned that, to have arrived at the position of challenger, I must have won some fights. They might have noted that, while the champion had failed to flatten Tom Gibbons, I had knocked him out. The prizefight "experts" were almost unanimous in not giving me a chance."

Tunney was disregarded as a legitimate threat to Dempsey by most leading experts in the field of boxing. To many, Tunney was basically just a blown-up light-heavyweight who lacked a killer instinct. He was unfairly frowned upon by critics who thought he lacked savage aggressiveness in the ring. To his credit, however, Tunney in fact won most of his fights by knockout. Amazingly, many boxing experts overlooked this significant statistic.

Teddy Hayes didn't like the idea of Dempsey getting in the ring with Tunney. He reasoned that Jack had not fought for three years and he was terribly rusty. Tunney could very well take the title away from Dempsey because of the long lay-off and because the ex-Marine was an outstanding boxer who had never been knocked down in his professional career. Moreover, Dempsey had shown that he had trouble in the ring with good boxers who knew how to neutralize Jack's attacks.

Dempsey ignored all of Teddy's warnings. He refused to consider statistics regarding past fights involving great fighters who had difficulty winning after a long lay-off. Jack assured his friend that the long layoff would not be a factor once he got back into shape. Teddy was not so sure about Dempsey's confidence. After all, Tunney beat Gibbons in twelve rounds, whereas Jack took the decision against Gibbons after fifteen hard fought rounds.

Rickard tried to set up a bout between Dempsey and Tunney but ran into some stiff headwinds. The New York State Athletic Commission refused to allow Rickard a chance to promote a Dempsey-Tunney fight in New York because Jack was under suspension. Rickard threatened the Commission that he would hold the fight in another state if they didn't lift the suspension against Jack.

Dempsey left Hollywood and Estelle in order to visit old friends in New York. Dempsey hung out with Billy Seeman. The two men were friends with New York Mayor Jimmy Walker. Seeman introduced Jack to all kinds of characters, including bootleggers, mobsters, models, and dancehall girls. Jack partied with Seeman at all hours of the night. One morning, Seeman woke Jack up much earlier than usual.

"There's an ambitious young kid out here," Seeman informed Dempsey, "who's been assigned by his paper to interview you. He's so jumpy you'd think he was about to interview Coolidge."

Dempsey slipped into his red robe and walked into the room where the young reporter from the *Graphic* was nervously waiting. The kid introduced himself as reporter Ed Sullivan. Sullivan was so jittery, he knocked over a chair in the process of introducing himself. Jack smiled and asked Ed not to be so nervous. Years later, Ed Sullivan confessed to Dempsey that he almost passed out from nervousness by just being in the champion's presence.

As soon as Estelle arrived in New York, the Dempseys moved into a hotel more suitable to Estelle's tastes. The pair starred in a Broadway play called *The Big Fight* which was scheduled to open at the Majestic theatre. Naturally, Dempsey headlined the show and received a very impressive payment of $1,250 a week. Estelle was very disappointed at her second billing status and received a mere $300 a week. Dempsey played a fighter named Tiger Jack Dillon and Estelle played a heroine named Shirley Moore. The plot involved a betting syndicate that tried to pressure the champion into taking a fall for one million dollars.

Dempsey grew weary of all the rehearsals. It was grueling under the hot lights and he lost as much weight rehearsing as he did training for a fight. David Belasco, the show's director, was not impressed with Dempsey's acting abilities. Dempsey was concerned that Belasco might walk off the set and leave the show stranded. He referred to Jack as the "concrete laden star of the show."

Kearns relentlessly filed more lawsuits against Dempsey. Teddy became very concerned about Jack's welfare. Dempsey had gained a lot of weight due to his lack of serious training and partying. Rickard tried to convince Dempsey to get back into the ring as soon as possible. Dempsey gave Rickard permission to arrange a bout between himself and Gene Tunney. Upon learning about the upcoming fight, Kearns met with Dempsey and warned him that he was still Jack's manager. Furthermore, Kearns was in the process of arranging a fight between Dempsey and Harry Wills. Dempsey informed Kearns that he was free to make his own career decisions. Dempsey graciously offered to keep Kearns on as manager but only if he agreed to a 33 percent cut of the winnings. Kearns, disgusted with Jack's apparent ingratitude, turned the offer down cold.

Kearns was convinced that Estelle had turned Jack

against him. He was certain Estelle would lead Dempsey
to ruin and despair. Jack was constantly woken up in the
middle of the night by crank callers. He was shocked to
discover the assets in his bank accounts had been frozen.
The rift between Teddy Hayes and Jack worsened and they
eventually broke off their partnership. To add insult to
injury, Hayes filed a lawsuit against Dempsey.

Jack had invested a lot of his money in real estate. He
was now in danger of losing much of it because he had not
defended his title in such a long time. Meanwhile, Rickard
continued to search for support for a Dempsey-Tunney
fight. He was facing stiff resistance because of the Harry
Wills controversy. Out of desperation, Rickard even tried
to set up a fight between Tunney and Wills. The deal fell
through when Wills allegedly demanded too much money.
When Rickard tried to establish Yankee Stadium as the
location for the Dempsey-Tunney fight, the boxing commission suspended his promoter's license.

Gene Normile and Dempsey scheduled a meeting
with Rickard to discuss prize money. Dempsey wanted a
$500,000 guarantee, and 50 percent of all earnings over
a million-dollar gate. He also wanted 51 percent of the
motion picture earnings.

Rickard spoke with Governor Small of Illinois about
the possibility of a Dempsey-Wills fight. He was concerned,
however, that Tunney would not be much of a draw. The
governor told Rickard that in no way would a Dempsey-
Wills fight take place in his state. Small was extremely concerned about possible race riots breaking out in cities like
Chicago.

Normile contacted Rickard and warned him that he

either arrange for the next Dempsey fight to be held out-side of New York or he would find a new promoter. He told Rickard that the committee running the Philadelphia Centennial was keenly interested in holding the fight in their city. Rickard promised Normile that he would try to strike a deal with Philadelphia as soon as possible.

Dempsey was ecstatic about the possibility of facing Tunney in Philadelphia. He left New York for Hollywood so that he could tell Estelle the great news. Estelle was not particularly happy to hear about Jack's next fight. She liked the fact that her husband could beat anyone in the ring, but she firmly believed he should quit the fight game. She was concerned about the possibility that her husband might get seriously injured in the ring. Jack explained to Estelle about how badly they needed the money. Estelle's film career had stalled and Dempsey was no longer collecting income from Universal. He was also paying lawyers to handle all the lawsuits Kearns kept slapping him with.

Dempsey hired Jerry the Greek as his trainer. Jerry the Greek was rightfully worried that Dempsey had not fought in three years. He was in the worst shape of his career and he was 31 years of age. Against his better judgment, Jerry the Greek agreed to help Jack train for the fight.

Gene Normile became increasingly aggravated about the guarantee Rickard had promised Dempsey. Normile was concerned that Kearns might be able to legally get a cut of the action from the proposed Dempsey-Tunney fight. The uncertainty surrounding Dempsey's earnings from the fight began to adversely affect Dempsey's state of mind. He was constantly approached by process servers. To help put an end to this encroachment, Normile hired body guards in order to keep undesirables away from Jack.

Kearns was absolutely relentless in his quest to unnerve Dempsey. He even went so far as to obtain a writ of attachment against Dempsey's Rolls Royce. Estelle, who had been driving the Rolls Royce, was approached one day by Kearns' operatives. She was ordered to remove herself from the automobile. Having no other means of transportation, she was forced to walk all the way back to Jack's training camp in Atlantic City.

Meanwhile, Normile and Dempsey decided to ask Rickard for an advancement of their guarantee. Rickard agreed, perhaps partly out of sympathy to Dempsey's physical condition. Jack was suffering from dermatitis, a condition possibly caused by a great deal of stress. Rickard suggested to Jack that he should postpone the fight. Dempsey was determined not to change the date of the fight because too many fight fans had already purchased tickets for the bout. More importantly, Dempsey felt that he could easily beat Tunney.

Jack advised Estelle to return home to California because she constantly fretted about his health and the possibility that he could get seriously hurt in the upcoming battle. She reluctantly agreed. With Estelle out of the way, Dempsey was now able to train hard for the fight. He drank large portions of olive oil to help his digestion immediately before retiring for bed.

Several days before the scheduled bout, a sheriff approached Normile at his Atlantic City residence and handed him a warrant for Jack's arrest. Henry Tobin, a notorious gambler, was with Normile at the time of the incident. The sheriff told Normile and Tobin that the bond was for one hundred thousand dollars. Tobin told the sheriff to come back in two hours and the money would be ready. The sheriff hesitantly agreed to the arrangement. Henry Tobin made three phone calls and within an hour the money was delivered to him. Dempsey remained oblivious regarding this incident until after the fight was over. He was also told after the fight that Kearns had served him with an alarming total of seven injunctions.

Dempsey, Jerry the Greek, and Normile traveled to Philadelphia by train on September 23. As the train approached the Broad Street Station in Philadelphia, Dempsey suddenly became violently ill. His legs felt like rubber and his stomach felt queasy. Sensing something was seriously wrong with Jack, Jerry the Greek yelled, "Mr. Normile, you better call the fight off!"

Normile quickly turned toward Dempsey, who was leaning against a door. His eyes were partially shut and he didn't recognize Normile at first.

"What's the matter, Jack," Normile asked Jack. "What is it, kid?"

Dempsey assured him that whatever it was, it wasn't something he couldn't deal with. On the way to the Sesquicentennial Municipal Stadium, Dempsey had to get out of the car several times so that he could vomit. Once they arrived at the stadium, Normile and Jerry the Greek helped Jack back on his feet. When they arrived at his dressing room, Jack had difficulty removing his shoes without falling over.

New York Times reporter, Paul Gallico, was not impressed with Dempsey's training sessions. He thought Jack looked lethargic. The champion didn't look anything like the Dempsey of old. He was not as fast on his feet as he once was and his punches lacked ferocity. He thought the challenger could very possibly "hand the experts the greatest shock of their careers by winning." Gallico, however, was speaking based on personal observation and not his heart. He disliked Tunney immensely and wanted to see the challenger knocked out.

"Every person I spoke to," he went on, "prayed fervently that Dempsey would knock his block off. Tunney's strutting, his blowing, his vain parading, have aroused a longing in the breasts of many to see his still form stretched beneath the white lamps."

Reporters asked Jack about his new nose and whether he was concerned about Tunney damaging it with one of his jabs. "I've urged my sparring partners to go for the nose," Dempsey replied, "and some of them have landed healthy socks. There's nothing to worry about. I breathe better through the nose now and it doesn't give under the strain of a hard punch. It hurts to get hit there, sure, but any nose hurts when it is hit."

Privately, Dempsey was concerned about his fight with Gene Tunney. He was well aware of the fact that he had not defended his title for several years. "Three years had passed since my battle with the Wild Bull of the Argentine," he recalled years later. "During that time I had boxed only in exhibition matches, for none of which any regular training was required. Tex Rickard's advice had been not to fight too often. He was thinking from the standpoint of the promoter, of greater spectacles and bigger gate receipts. In accepting his point of view I let myself get farther and farther from the ring condition necessary to prove myself still champion of the world. At the same time, I wasn't getting any younger."

Dempsey was keenly aware of the tragic fate of other great heavyweight champions who returned to the ring after a long layoff, only to be ultimately defeated. "No champion can lie back for years," he later recounted, "and retain his crown. Jim Corbett, master boxer, supremely confident of his ability to whip all comers, failed to whip all comers, failed to defend his title for three years — and then lost it to "Ruby Robert" Fitzsimmons, nearly 30 pounds lighter than he. Jim Jeffries, one of the mightiest of them all, retired undefeated, only to find that, after a layoff of years, he couldn't come back. Jess Willard felt it unnecessary to defend the championship for three years before he fought me, and he let himself in for a rough awakening."

Gene Tunney initially trained at a remote resort somewhere in the Adirondacks. Tunney's road work included jogging backwards while throwing punches. He frequently threw a hard right cross in the air because he knew Jack was vulnerable to that type of punch. He also knew the only way he could beat the champion was to avoid being on the receiving end of a savage, Dempsey assault.

According to Dempsey, Tex Rickard and Jack discussed the real possibility of postponing his proposed fight with Tunney. Jack was concerned that his troubles with Kearns' lawsuits and his deteriorating health might adversely affect his chances of defeating Tunney. Rickard reminded Jack that a rather large amount of tickets for the fight had already been sold. Rickard convinced Dempsey that he shouldn't have any problem defeating Tunney. Jack decided that Tex was probably right about his chances of retaining the heavyweight title and allowed the fight to go on as scheduled.

After the announcement that the fight would definitely take place in Philadelphia, Tunney moved his training camp to Stroudsburg, Pennsylvania. Tunney drew many young women to his training camp. A society writer wrote that "Hundreds of girls who take their vacations in September have come to the country to get a peep at their hero. And Gene has a smile for all, a handshake, too, and his signature when he cannot do otherwise."

"It would be difficult," the writer continued, "to find a more perfect Adonis type, every feature being correct. In a measure, his photographs reveal this; and perhaps that is another reason why he is the recipient of such an extraordinary amount of 'mash' mail. From all parts of the country, they write him, with some of his admirers being most persistent."

Tunney made a point of sparring with some of Jack's old sparring partners. He asked them to provide clues about the champion's flaws. After a few rounds of sparring, Tunney could be seen sitting under a tree reading classic literature or playing a few rounds of golf. Tunney made it a practice every day to spar with a man whom he had some difficulty defeating in two of his previous fights. The fighter, Jimmy Delaney, had defeated many outstanding heavyweights. Tunney chose Delaney partly because he was similar to Dempsey in several respects. He fought out of a crouch and he possessed a very effective left hook.

Many celebrities were polled in order to determine who they thought would win the Dempsey-Tunney bout. Ty Cobb, tennis star Bill Tilden, Yankee slugger Lou Gehrig, and New York Giants baseball manager, John

McGraw, all came out in favor of Dempsey retaining the title. Babe Ruth refused to voice his opinion. He may have been despondent over the fact that the heavyweight champion was more popular than he was. At one time, Ruth even considered becoming a prizefighter. Like many sports stars who considered boxing as a career, Ruth quickly gave up the notion when he discovered just how brutal and dangerous the sport actually was.

Less than ten percent of those who were asked to pick the favorite gave Tunney the nod. Philadelphia Jack O'Brien, the former lightweight champion, liked the challenger's chances. "I like the way Tunney moves and counters and thinks on his feet," O'Brien explained. "I respect Dempsey but I like Tunney one hundred percent."

Jack, like most boxing fans, didn't think much of Gene Tunney's chances of winning the heavyweight title. "Tunney was just a boxer," Dempsey kept telling himself. "That was about the only comforting thing I could think of in those busy days leading up to the fight. I'd move in through those light punches and flatten him as soon as I caught him. Who the hell was Tunney? Sure, I knew all about how he prepared for this chance over the years, how he took special exercises to increase the size of his neck and make him able to take a punch better, how he used to carry sponge balls in each hand night and day, working and gripping them to make his hands bigger and stronger. And I knew he was a Marine. So did the crowd. There were boos for me."

Harry Greb, the only fighter ever to have beaten Gene Tunney, was absolutely convinced Gene would beat the champion. Referring to Tunney, Greb told reporters, "That fellow is far better than you scribes believe. Make no mistake about that, he'll whip Dempsey." Scoffed at by one reporter regarding his absurd prediction, Greb shot back. "Don't make a fool of yourself," he advised. "Dempsey will be lucky to win a round. I know because I've worked with Dempsey and I have boxed Tunney. Tunney has just the stuff to beat Dempsey and do it all the way. If Dempsey beats him, it will be an accident."

Mickey Walker, former welterweight champion, believed Tunney had almost no chance of taking the title away from Jack. Walker and Kearns put up a lot of money betting Dempsey would win. Walker later remarked that "We figured we had a sucker's money. The odds on Dempsey ranged from four-to -one to seven-to-one. The only knowledgeable fight man I knew who was smart enough to take the short end was Harry Greb, who put ten thousand dollars on Tunney. Greb had inside knowledge of their styles. He had worked out with Jack in gyms and had fought Gene five times, beating him only once. Harry came to me before the fight. 'Mickey,' he said, 'bet on Tunney. He's going to beat Dempsey. He has real boxing ability, he has the tools, he's classy, a much better fighter than anybody imagines.' Like almost everybody else, I didn't believe him."

The Dempsey-Tunney fight drew approximately 120,000 paying customers. Scattered among the vast crowd were tycoons, politicians, gangsters, and Hollywood celebrities. Rickard, displaying his flair for brilliant promotion, famously dubbed the bout as the "Battle of the Century."

Dempsey recalled an incident regarding an associate named Mike Jacobs. "Years later Mike told of being approached on the day of the fight by Boo Boo Hoff, the Philadelphia mob fellow, who said he had to have twenty-five more ringside seats to take care of his friends in Philadelphia and Pennsylvania politics. Mike said the whole ringside was sold out. Boo Boo shook his head. 'I've got to get them,' he said. He pulled out a roll that would choke an elephant and counted off twenty-five $1,000 bills and handed them to Mike. Mike made some quick changes in the ringside, moving in chairs, moving people who wouldn't gripe too much, handed over the twenty-five tickets and pocketed the $25,000. Boo Boo put the tickets in his pocket and started away. 'Just a minute,' Mike said in his crabby way. 'You forgot to pay me for the tickets. They're fifty bucks each.' And Boo Boo paid. You couldn't hold a big fight in those days without doing some kind of business with the mob in charge of the town."

Tunney carefully studied all of Dempsey's fight films. Like all great boxers, he noticed significant flaws in his opponent's style of fighting. He noticed, for example, that both Carpentier and Firpo landed several overhead rights to Jack's head as the champion charged forward. In fact, Dempsey was knocked out of the ring by Firpo with a kind of half-punch, half shove. Tunney observed that Jack had difficulty fighting experienced boxers like Tommy Gibbons. Gibbons was able to last fifteen rounds by cleverly out-boxing the champion.

Tunney entered the ring at around 9:30 pm to a huge ovation. He wore a robe with a Marine insignia proudly displayed. The champion climbed into the ring four minutes later. Surprisingly, he was met with as many boos as cheers. This may have been partly due to the fact that he had spent an inordinate amount of time away from the ring, thus depriving many boxing fans the opportunity of experiencing brutal savagery. Tunney looked supremely confident, as if he knew how the bout would play out. Tunney stood in his corner smiling and nodding his head. Dempsey, on the other hand, stood in his corner unshaven and scowling at no one in particular.

Gene Tunney took his time wrapping his hands with bandages. Dempsey had kept him waiting and now it was Gene's turn to make the champion wait as well. Tunney even joked with Dempsey's seconds, Jack O'Brien and Gus Wilson. He kidded that they were "seconding a loser tonight."

Ring announcer Joe Griffo introduced Dempsey to the crowd as "the heavyweight champion who had defended his title for the past six years." Many in the crowd understandably took exception to the announcer's overstatement. They vigorously booed Griffo's statement. After the outburst subsided, referee Tommy Reilly called both fighters to the center of the ring for prefight instructions. As the two combatants returned to their respective corners, the challenger said to the champion, "May the better man win, Jack." Dempsey appeared somewhat confused by Tunney's assertion.

The two fighters were a study in contrasts. Tunney appeared totally calm while Dempsey looked nervous and unsure of himself. In the back of Jack's mind were thoughts that perhaps someone might walk up to him and shove a warrant in his face.

As the bell sounded for round one, Dempsey rushed toward Tunney with a vengeance. He backed Tunney into the ropes and landed a hard right on the challenger's cheek. Dempsey continued stalking Tunney, trying to land power punches to Gene's face and body. Suddenly, Tunney unleashed a wicked right to Dempsey's chin, stunning the champion. As Dempsey continued to stalk Tunney, the challenger rushed Jack and caught him with a flurry of punches. The round ended and Dempsey slowly walked back to his corner. Tunney looked fresh and confident. Jack tried to hide the fact that he had been badly shaken by Tunney's unexpected onslaught.

Tunney later recalled that by retreating from Jack's stalking, he wanted the champion to think that he was terrified of Dempsey. Gene later claimed that "I wanted him to become a little overconfident." Another tactic Tunney used against Dempsey was his ability to fall into a clinch after each Dempsey assault. Tunney recalled that the sneaky right hand he used to hit the champion with high on the cheekbone was devastating. "He was stopped in his tracks and his knees sagged," Tunney proudly recalled. "Perhaps if the punch landed on Jack's jaw, I might have knocked him out." Dempsey's low crouching style of fighting may very well have saved him from being knocked out.

Dempsey was so shaken by Gene's punch to the head that he may not have recovered from it throughout the rest of the fight. The right hand that landed squarely on Dempsey's cheek bone was, according to Tunney, "the hardest right I've ever thrown." The blow clearly hurt Dempsey, but his uncanny ability to take a vicious punch saved him from a knock down, and very possibly from a knockout as well.

"Here was my first fight against Bill Brennan, in reverse," Dempsey recounted in his book, *Round By Round.* "Instead of my having landed the first blow against a formidable opponent, softening him up for the entire fight, Gene Tunney had handed it to me. All through the round he outboxed me, landing a lot of good blows. I tried not to let him see how badly I had been shaken up. I was even able to fool a good many of the reporters at the ringside. Only a few of them wrote that I was barely able to weather the round."

Jerry the Greek frantically held salts under Jack's nose as the champion perked up. No amount of smelling salts, however, could help alleviate the weakness Jack felt in his legs. Dempsey suddenly felt very old. He knew he was up against a superior boxer who could also punch. Jack's confidence was shattered and he was not sure if he could last ten rounds. Yet somehow he felt he must successfully defend the title at all costs because so many of his closest friends and fans expected him to win. He was groggy from the unexpected pounding he received from Tunney. It was vitally important for Jack not to appear weak. If Gene sensed that Jack was in trouble, he would attack the champion even more. Dempsey had not seen many of the punches Tunney had thrown at him and that worried him.

After the first round, it was apparent how the rest of the fight might proceed. Dempsey would charge Tunney from the opening gong and Gene would retreat, moving clockwise in order to lessen the impact of a murderous left hook by Dempsey. Gene successfully landed overhead rights to Dempsey's face and then quickly backpedaled in order to avoid another attack by the champion. Tunney stood erect and at times leaned backwards. He refused to go on the attack because that might open himself up to a frontal assault by the champion.

In round two Dempsey wasted no time attacking Tunney. He landed a hard right to Tunney's jaw. Tunney didn't appear hurt at all by Dempsey's punch. The challenger answered Dempsey's attack with a swift combination of lefts and rights. Tunney landed a perfect right-cross to Dempsey's jaw just as the bell sounded ending the round. Dempsey appeared somewhat exhausted while Tunney looked sharp. Many boxing experts and sportswriters were utterly amazed that Gene was confident enough to get close to Dempsey so that he could exchange blows with the Manassa Mauler.

In round three Dempsey approached Tunney slowly and cautiously. Apparently, Tunney's blows were taking a terrific toll on Jack. Dempsey was particularly bothered by the fact that Tunney's punches were finding their target while at the same time his punches were missing completely. Tunney boxed brilliantly while Dempsey threw wild punches in the air, tiring himself out in the process. He was aiming at Gene's jaw, hoping for a miracle knockout. Tunney retaliated with a left and right to the chin. Tunney landed a solid blow to Jack's left eye. Blood began to flow from the cut. Tunney, sensing the end may be near, threw several more punches to Dempsey's jaw. Jack looked hurt and confused.

"Between the third and fourth rounds," Dempsey recalled years later, "I gave myself "Doc" Kearns' old command: 'Pull up your socks you big bum!' As I came from my corner I tried to fight harder, as I had been able to against Bill Brennan the first time my title seemed to be slipping. I charged into Gene before he could get to the center of the ring and sent him to the ropes with a hard right and left to the head. When he managed to pull away from me, I rushed again and landed a right to the jaw. But this time Gene countered with a good right, and followed it with a stiff uppercut that shook me up. When I rushed again he sidestepped neatly while my momentum carried me helplessly past him."

Graham McNamee announced to his radio listeners that "We will have to tell you that Tunney has now won three rounds." The public perception held that Dempsey would surely knock out the relatively unknown challenger inside five rounds. McNamee further stated to a shocked nation that Tunney "is out boxing the champion from start to finish. Dempsey is absolutely unable to get going. He seems to have nothing, except that now and then he shoots over a left."

Tunney totally controlled the fight in the fourth round. As soon as Jack threw a punch, Tunney retreated, clinched, counterpunched, or quickly sidestepped away from any retaliation. McNamee explained to his radio audience that "Dempsey seems to be satisfied to take all the punches, anything to get in on Tunney, while standing flatfooted in the middle of the ring. It is a very tame round, and once again Tunney shows his superiority. Tunney has now won four rounds in succession."

Round five was very similar to the previous four rounds. Tunney continued to pummel Jack with flurries of punches. The champion simply could not adequately defend himself against Tunney's blows. Dempsey was growing increasingly tired. He tried to corner Tunney, but the challenger either side-stepped, back-pedaled, or clinched his way out of potentially dangerous situations.

It was becoming very obvious to Dempsey during the fifth round that his title was slipping away. The more Jack pressed Tunney, the more Gene tied Jack up. Jack thought all he could realistically do for the remainder of the fight was to avoid losing by a knock out. He understood the only way he could defeat Tunney was by landing a flurry of ferocious punches to Gene's jaw. He knew the chance of that happening, however, was slim.

Dempsey recounted later that Gene refused to press him throughout the fight. Tunney was completely satisfied with counterpunching and clinching whenever Jack attacked him. Dempsey thought Gene's ring strategy was sound. On the other hand, Jack felt that by Tunney acting safe, he missed an opportunity of knocking him out. In Jack's view, Tunney was more interested in winning the fight by a unanimous decision then he was by taking chances and attacking Jack, thereby allowing himself to get close to the champion and perhaps getting tagged in the process.

While Dempsey and Tunney were going at it in the sixth round, "Doc" Kearns turned to an associate and sadly related, "He's gonna lose. His timing's off and his legs are gone. Still, there's something he could do." Mark Kelly, a sportswriter for a Los Angeles newspaper advised Kearns to go over to Dempsey's corner and help him. "The guys in there aren't any good at all," Kelly explained. Shaking his head, Kearns rejected Kelly's suggestion. "No. Let him take it," Kearns replied. "That's the way he wanted it and that's the way it will have to be."

Dempsey blamed the wet ring for his slowness. "I was slower than I thought or Tunney was faster," Dempsey recounted later. "I was blaming the wet ring but it didn't bother Tunney. He glided around like a skater on ice." As soon as Jack gained traction, Tunney was suddenly out of range from Dempsey's potential haymakers. Tunney constantly battered Jack's face with left jabs, causing him to be off-balance much of the fight. In a desperate attempt to land a big blow to end the fight or at least hurt Tunney, Jack left himself open to stiff rights. He was slow-footed throughput much of the bout. Jack never mounted an effective response to any of Tunney's attacks.

The tenth round began as the heavy rain continued to drench all in attendance. Dempsey was fully aware that he desperately needed to knock out Tunney in order to keep the title. Each time Dempsey rushed the challenger, Tunney landed vicious rights and lefts to Dempsey's face. Tunney concentrated his attacks on Dempsey's head as the round ended. The champion's face was swollen and badly cut up and almost totally unrecognizable.

The torrential downpour added a kind of sickening surrealism to the fight. It was difficult for Dempsey supporters to accept the fact that their hero had been beaten convincingly by a relatively unknown fighter. Ringside announcer Graham McNamee said that it was a "sorrowful sight" to see the best fighter from his generation look "like a novice."

After Tunney was declared the clear winner, Dempsey felt thoroughly disgusted with himself. He approached Tunney, put his weary arm around the new champion, and congratulated the victor. "Gene, you're a great champion," he said. "Lots of luck to you." Jack turned around and walked to his corner and then something occurred that surprised Jack. The crowd cheered Dempsey as if he had won the fight. The ex-champion believed that at that moment, "losing was the making of me." "You'll always be the champion," one man yelled up to the defeated Dempsey. "You're our champion forever."

In his book, *The Million Dollar Gate*, Kearns revealed

his thoughts about the fight and about Jack. "By the fourth round I knew, and by the sixth round it was quite clear, that Dempsey was the loser. Tunney, a master boxer, was in faultless physical condition. Dempsey hadn't fought since beating Firpo, three years and three months earlier, and obviously wasn't in anything like the shape I had always demanded."

Kearns claimed Dempsey would have been in far better shape had he been Jack's manager at the time of the Dempsey-Tunney fight. The professional relationship between the two men, however, had been severely damaged. "No matter what comes between two people," Kearns wrote, "if they have fought hard times together and made good it doesn't all disappear. But Dempsey had called the shot and, without him having asked me, my pride wouldn't let me budge. I sat there watching him take his licking and, as Kelly said, it wasn't all rain that was running down my cheeks. Because this Dempsey was a caricature of the tiger I had fashioned – a man who fought Tunney's fight, and had nobody to prod and needle him into making it go his way. When it was over I went out and got drunk."

Grantland Rice wrote in his autobiography that, at the end, "Dempsey's face was a beaten mask that Tunney had torn up like a ploughed field. Speed of foot, a sharp jab and a right cross that ripped Dempsey's face like a can opener were going for Tunney that night against a man who, despite a rocky training period, had been installed a 4 and 5 to one favorite. Tunney, at twenty-nine, had arrived on his toes. Dempsey, at thirty-one, departed flat-footed. Dempsey had never been knocked out, but had the fight gone fifteen rounds, the referee would have had to stop it."

The defeated world heavyweight champion told

reporters after the fight that "the people were cheering for me, calling out my name in a way I had never heard before. I never realized how much I had hungered for a sound like that, and now here it was — on the night I blew my title."

In comparison, Gene Tunney's ovation was muted. He received polite applause but that was it. Clean Gene the Marine may have felt somewhat let down by boxing fans in Sesquicentennial Municipal Stadium that historic night. Later in his dressing room, he explained to the sportswriters that he thought Dempsey was doomed to lose based on what had happened to him in the very first round.

Both judges awarded all ten rounds to Gene Tunney. The fight was unique in that it was the first time a fighter from the Empire State had become heavyweight champion of the world. Also, it was the first time a heavyweight title changed hands via a decision.

By most accounts, Tunney had won all ten rounds of the fight. The only time Dempsey caught fire was when he hit Tunney's throat with a hard left hook in the sixth round. The blow was so powerful, Tunney coughed up blood. Dempsey was incapable, however, of mounting any kind of offence.

Many boxing critics blamed Dempsey's beating on his handlers. Paul Gallico thought Jack hadn't taken the fight seriously enough while training for the bout. A reporter for the *Chicago Tribune* was thoroughly convinced that Dempsey's fast living and film acting had done him in during the last three and a half years. Damon Runyon was of the opinion that Jack's legal battles with Kearns weighed heavily on Dempsey's mind.

For weeks, sportswriters had a field day blasting

Dempsey's lackadaisical performance against the newly crowned champion. One reporter wrote: "In defeat, Dempsey was revealed as an overrated fighter, a man who was good, but never great." He was accused of taking the title away from an out of shape, bumbling Jess Willard, a seriously ill Billy Miske, and a totally overrated Frenchman, Georges Carpentier. He was incapable of knocking out an above average boxer like Tommy Gibbons, and he almost lost the title to an unknown, clumsy brawler like Luis Angel Firpo.

Dempsey was deeply hurt when he read some of the scathing comments about his defeat. "Let me tell you," Dempsey explained, "I was licked by a darn good fighter, and I only wish that some of the guys who say Tunney can't hit could sample the first smash I got at the very start of the fight. There was plenty of sock, and I never really got over it through the rest of the fight."

Jack was livid about being accused of not giving it his all against Tunney. "That is the one thing that hurt me more than any of Gene's punches," Dempsey was quoted as saying. "Some of the guys who I thought were my pals said things in their stories that cut me deep. There's always a lot of funny talk after a big fight, but some of the boys I have in mind ought to know me well enough to know that I'd give my right arm to keep the championship."

Many boxing experts theorized that Jack Dempsey in his prime would have soundly defeated Tunney at his peak. After all, they contended, no one could withstand the kind of punishment Dempsey dished out while he was either at or near his prime. There are those, however, who argued that Jack had trouble with outstanding boxers like Tommy Gibbons and Gene Tunney. They further claimed that he only did exceptionally well against big, burly fighters like Carl Morris and Jess Willard. Big, powerful fighters were made to order for Dempsey, his critics argued.

Tunney, on the other hand, was a ring general, astute in the art of defense as well as offense. He knew better than anyone how to protect himself in the ring. He side-stepped, back-pedaled, and clinched his way out of potential trouble by the likes of a Jack Dempsey.

After the bout, Tunney spoke with the press and offered up some insights about his fight with the dethroned champion. "I had made up my mind I'd win. I aimed to prove to the skeptics that I was worthy of the match. I was tired of the criticism aimed at me by the press. I knew my capability and went into the ring determined to prove that I was a worthy contender."

Tunney explained to the press how he prepared for the title fight. He described in detail how closely he studied Dempsey's style of fighting. "In his fight with Firpo," Tunney related, "Jack revealed himself an open target for a vicious punch. But he displayed tremendous hitting power, speed, and endurance. I made a close study of all these points and decided that Dempsey was not an invincible target as most reporters had written. My scrutiny of Jack's good and weak points is what enabled me to win the title."

In Tunney's book, *Arms for Living*, he further explained how the Dempsey-Carpentier fight helped him understand more about Dempsey's strengths and weaknesses. "I saw the vicious attack, shifty stalking, the elusive bobbing, the swift sliding in, the short, heavy punches, the damaging body blows-they impressed me! To me it was obvious that Carpentier, light and inferior in punching power, was going to be defeated when Dempsey caught up with him. In that bout, I learned a lot. I decided I could hit Dempsey with short right-hand punches that would hurt him. That was confirmed when Jack fought Firpo. That, I figured, was Dempsey's weakness."

Estelle called Jack and asked him what had happened. "Honey. I just forgot to duck," Dempsey replied. Jack's response to Estelle endeared him to countless sports fans throughout the world. His popularity soared and his legend was now beginning to take hold. Decades later, President Ronald Reagan would jokingly respond with the same quip to a reporter's question after nearly being assassinated by John Hinkley in 1981.

Tunney heaped praise upon the fallen heavyweight king. "Dempsey fought like the great champion he was," the new champion proclaimed. "He had the kick of a mule in his fists and the heart of a lion in his breast. I never fought a harder socker nor do I hope to meet one. I'm content to rest a while with the ambition I have for seven years finally realized."

After Tunney became the world's heavyweight champion, George Bernard Shaw befriended Gene. They corresponded frequently with each other. Tunney was given permission to lecture on William Shakespeare's plays at the highly prestigious Yale University. After winning the title, it appeared to many that Tunney was suddenly an authority on the classics and needed to be heard.

Dempsey responded graciously to the new heavyweight champion of the world. "I have no alibis to offer. I lost to a good man, an American. A man who speaks the English language. I have no alibis." One would have to wonder what the Frenchman Georges Carpentier thought about Dempsey's comments. Gene Normile issued a statement on behalf of the ex-champion. "I am glad," the statement read, "that the championship has passed into the hands of an American and a fine fighter. I wish him the best of luck."

CHAPTER EIGHT

DEMPSEY VS TUNNEY II

Dempsey stands over fallen champion Gene Tunney in their rematch in 1927. Tunney had never been knocked down prior to this title fight.

Dempsey announced his retirement from the fight game. He knew he had been beaten quite convincingly by a man he was certain he could destroy. Jack recognized that he was no longer newsworthy. Sportswriters who had once idolized Dempsey were now noticeably avoiding him.

The ex-champ was certain his career in the ring was over. He had lost every round to a boxer he was supposed to have easily knocked out in the early rounds of the fight. For the first time in his boxing career, he was concerned about his health. The great Sam Langford, the fighter Dempsey had wisely ducked early in his career, had succumbed to blindness. Langford had been hit in the face countless times during his spectacular career. Ex-champion Harry Greb suffered from bad vision and eventually died after undergoing eye surgery. He was only thirty-two when he unexpectedly passed away. Circumstances such as these weighed heavily on Dempsey's mind.

Jack thought long and hard about his fight with Tunney. Had the three year lay-off been too much for him to overcome? He also took into account the fact that his punching power and stamina had noticeably declined. If he were to fight Tunney again, would he be fast enough to catch Tunney at a vulnerable moment and knock him out? These are questions Dempsey must surely have asked himself repeatedly.

Jack reflected back to the time when he won the heavyweight championship title from Jess Willard. After winning the title he felt a sense of doom because the only direction left for him was down. He relished the fact that he had held the title longer than any previous heavyweight champion. He also felt very proud that he had participated in all three million-dollar gates.

Back in Hollywood, Dempsey agonized over his future while Estelle fretted over her career. With nothing promising on the horizon, Jack decided to sell real estate for a living. Tex Rickard pleaded with Dempsey to consider making a comeback. Jack refused to entertain the thought of ever fighting again. Rickard recognized that Jack didn't need the money, but he also knew that boxing had been Dempsey's whole life.

Jack started to work out in the gymnasium because he was concerned about gaining too much weight. Estelle warned him not to get back into the ring because she was afraid he might get seriously injured. She also abhorred the type of people Jack associated with. In February 1927, Dempsey was treated for blood poisoning. Jack's eyes had a strange yellow hue and he had lost eighteen pounds. Dempsey felt like he might die. He eventually recuperated from the ailment.

Kearns and Dempsey officially ended their partnership in the spring of 1927. Kearns took 100 percent ownership of the Wilshire Apartments and Dempsey acquired full ownership of the Barbara Hotel. The lawsuits leveled against Dempsey remained open, nevertheless. Kearns was determined to remain a thorn in Jack's side indefinitely.

One evening Babe Ruth stopped by Jack's house unannounced. The two sports superstars first met in 1921. They had closely watched each other's careers blossom. Ruth laid it on the line with Dempsey.

"Listen, Jack. You lost your crown while still on your feet. Sure, it's tough, but don't you think you owe yourself and your fans one more crack?"

"No, Babe," Jack replied. "I know when I'm through."

Ruth continued to badger Dempsey, telling him that all he was doing was sitting on his ass and feeling sorry for himself.

"Babe, I don't know if I've got it, see?" Jack explained.

"Well, goddamn it," Ruth shot back. "You won't know till you get out there and try!"

Dempsey and Ruth discussed the slugger's tape-measure home runs and his other accomplishments outside the sport. Before he left, Babe tried to explain to Dempsey the importance of returning to the ring in order to regain the heavyweight title. Jack remained unmoved by Ruth's well intentioned suggestion.

In the meantime, Tex Rickard continued to explain to Dempsey the advantages of fighting Tunney again.

"Naw, I ain't interested," Dempsey responded. "I'm through with the fight game, Tex. Over the hill, I guess."

"Well maybe you're right, kid. Maybe Tunney's too tough for you. No one likes to get licked by the same guy twice."

Somehow Rickard finally persuaded Dempsey to start training so he could get in shape. He told Jack that perhaps he could arrange a tune-up fight with someone before facing Tunney. Jack started training seriously in the vicinity of Ojai, California. He trained six days a week and came home every Sunday to be with Estelle. Now that Rickard had persuaded Jack to at least think about the possibility of returning to the ring, he began to consider another Tunney-Dempsey fight. Rickard was of the opinion that enough of the public believed Dempsey should have won the fight if he had not suffered from such a long layoff. They also recognized that Kearns had been threatening him for years with lawsuits and possible jail time for good measure. Rickard was aware that Dempsey and Tunney attended the Maloney-de Kuh fight and Dempsey received a much more spirited ovation from the crowd than did the champion. Rickard was determined to turn those cheers into ticket sales.

Determined to get back into his fighting weight, Jack trained every day. He was flabby and weighed about 227 pounds. He chopped trees, jumped rope, carried heavy rocks and climbed trees. He performed all these exercises under a great deal of pressure. He never knew when Rickard might call on him for his next fight.

By June of 1927, Dempsey had slimmed down considerably. He now weighed a remarkable 205 pounds. Dempsey moved his training camp to Soper's Ranch way up in the Ventura Mountains. Sportswriters began showing up during his training sessions like days of old. They were curious to see what kind of shape the ex-champion was in.

Dempsey assumed that his next fight would be a rubber match against Tunney. After all, Dempsey was under the impression along with many others that he may have lost to Tunney due to his three-year layoff. Tex Rickard had other ideas. He wanted Dempsey to fight the winner of a contest between "Sailor" Jack Sharkey and Jim Maloney.

Sharkey easily defeated Maloney by knocking him out in the fifth round. The winner of that fight would now face Dempsey. Rickard announced that the winner of the Dempsey-Sharkey fight would face Tunney for the heavyweight title. Rickard thought that Dempsey needed to beat

Sharkey in order to add legitimacy to a second Tunney-Dempsey fight. It was also a great way for Rickard to make even more money by capitalizing on Dempsey's popularity with fight fans.

Manager Leo Flynn advised Dempsey that Jack Sharkey was beatable because he was overconfident. He admitted that the Lithuanian was a terrific puncher and an excellent boxer, and he had an outstanding record. He had beaten several top heavyweight contenders including Mike McTigue, Johnny Risko, and the highly admired Harry Wills. Sharkey's victory over Wills was marred by the fact that he had won by a foul.

Dempsey began gaining some of his confidence back. He was convinced he was ready to face whomever Tex Rickard had in mind for his next battle. Jack called Rickard and told him to go ahead and arrange a fight between him and a respectable opponent. Shortly afterwards, Rickard informed Dempsey that he would definitely be facing Jack Sharkey in the ring on July 21, 1927, in New York. Dempsey was surprised how quickly Rickard arranged the match.

Jack explained to newspaper reporters that he was coming back "because I want to fight. It's my business. I'm not dead by a jugful." It appeared that Dempsey was throwing caution to the winds with his decision to return to the ring. Indeed, Tex Rickard himself might have believed that Jack could beat the rough and tough Jack Sharkey. "You can take Sharkey," Rickard advised Dempsey. "Just be careful of his left." Dempsey held a press conference in New York in which he pronounced to reporters, "I want to be convinced I'm wrong and that my ring days are over. Maybe Sharkey can convince me."

Tex Rickard hired Leo P. Flynn to be Dempsey's fight manager. Dempsey remembered Flynn from the days when he used to manage Bill Brennan. Flynn instructed Jack on everything from dawn to dusk. The first day the two men met they discussed the best way to go after Sharkey. Flynn erroneously claimed that Sharkey was a better fighter than Tunney. He advised Jack that Sharkey's only weakness was his inability to take body shots. "When you get in there," Flynn explained to Dempsey, "you keep punching to the body until he drops his hands. When he drops them, let that right hand go and then the left and knock him out."

Rickard arranged for Dempsey and Sharkey to meet at Madison Square Garden's ice skating rink. Dempsey was annoyed by Sharkey's cockiness and avoided him as much as possible. Flynn insisted that Dempsey should train in private until he appeared in better condition. He understood that bad press could negatively affect the gate. Lou Fink, Tunney's trainer, managed to watch Dempsey train. He was not impressed with Jack in the least. He thought the ex-champion was simply a shell of his former self and that Tunney should be able to beat him even more convincingly should the two meet again.

Dempsey received some horrible news during a training session. His brother, Johnny, had committed suicide. Johnny had been a drug addict for several years. He also deeply resented the fact that he stood in the shadow of his famous brother, Jack Dempsey, the world heavyweight champion. Jack immediately made arrangements for his brother's funeral. It also fell upon him to be the bearer of bad news to his parents.

History would be made on July 21, 1927, thanks

primarily to the drawing power of Jack Dempsey. 84,000 fans created the first million-dollar gate for a non-titled fight. The bout would take place at Yankee Stadium in New York. Because of Jack's tremendous popularity among sports fans, the Dempsey-Sharkey fight would have the largest radio hookup of all time. An estimated forty-eight radio stations allowed thirty million radio listeners to hear the broadcast. Amazingly, the hookup turned out to be even more expansive than the one covering Charles Lindbergh's return flight from Europe.

Jack Sharkey was supremely confident he could beat Dempsey. He told reporters just before the fight: "I am going in there to knock out Jack Dempsey." Sharkey was an 8-to-5 favorite going into the fight. The odds seemed reasonable to any sane boxing expert. Sharkey was an up and coming prospect for the heavyweight title. Jack had not only lost his last fight, but he had not defended his title for years. Sharkey may not have been as cagey and as quick as Tunney, but he could box circles around Jack and he could punch.

The media buildup leading into the fight was enormous. Sportswriters claimed that this fight could quite possibly be Dempsey's last battle. *New York Times* reporter James Dawson wrote: "The magnet of Dempsey, combined with the popularity Sharkey has attracted to himself through his rush to heavyweight prominence, is expected to make this the greatest non-championship battle in pugilistic history."

Unsurprisingly, the fight drew many dignitaries and celebrities from all over the world. Damon Runyon wrote that while he was attempting to take a seat near ringside, he "fell under the hurrying hoofs of fourteen kings of finance, twenty-nine merchant princes, six bootleggers, and five ticket speculators...all owners of Rolls Royce cars." Franklin Delano Roosevelt, now suffering from the debilitating effects of polio, was seated near ringside.

Dempsey received a tremendous ovation as he entered the ring. He looked confident and in remarkably good shape for someone who had fought only once in the previous three years. As Jack stood in his corner waiting nervously for the fight to begin, he thought about his chances. He had come to the conclusion that Sharkey was as fine a boxer as he had ever witnessed. According to Dempsey, Sharkey had the reflexes and movement of a good middleweight. He actually feared that he might get knocked out by Sharkey.

In the first round, Sharkey landed long bomb shells from both fists. Both fighters traded punches at very close quarters. Sharkey apparently disregarded his corner's advice and refused to just box with Dempsey. Perhaps he recognized how ineffective Dempsey's blows were and therefore decided to try and knock out Jack. Dempsey kept to his plan, however. He aggressively attacked Sharkey's body until his opponent grew weak and lowered his hands in an effort to protect his mid-section from further injury. Dempsey took a lot of punishment from Sharkey in the process. Sharkey hit Jack with a vicious left hook that split open Dempsey's lower lip. Blood streamed down his chin as he tried to defend himself. Sharkey smashed Dempsey in the jaw, causing Jack to wobble just as the bell sounded ending the round.

In the second round, Jack landed several hard left hooks

just as Sharkey was approaching him. Sharkey appeared to be unfazed by the blows, but Jack was certain the punches hurt the younger fighter. Meanwhile, Sharkey was pulling ahead of Dempsey on points. He hammered away at Dempsey's head and body almost at will. Jack left himself wide open as he tried to get inside in order to land some short-range punches. Dempsey later told reporters about how close he came to being knocked out early in the fight.

"He couldn't miss me with his left," Jack informed reporters. "He moved like a good middleweight. I thought he was going to knock me out." *New York Times* reporter, James P. Dawson wrote that Jack looked "slow and awkward, cumbersome, still and [he] has not a remnant of his former fighting speed and agility left." As Dempsey returned to his corner after the fourth round he looked thoroughly exhausted. He suffered from cuts around both eyes and his face was smeared with blood.

In the fifth round, Sharkey smashed Dempsey in the head with several hard blows. Jack struggled to stay on his feet. His entire body wobbled for a few seconds as if he was ready to hit the canvas for good. Sharkey made the horrible mistake of not finishing him off. Somehow, Dempsey miraculously managed to recuperate in a matter of seconds and continued to swarm all over an alarmed Sharkey. Sharkey's manager, Johnny Buckley, was ecstatic when he saw his fighter nearly put Dempsey away for good. Jack sensed, however, that Sharkey may have begun to lose energy in the fifth round. Dempsey's body blows appeared to have taken a terrible toll on the younger challenger.

Jack began to doubt the strategy of focusing his attack primarily on Sharkey's body. Flynn advised Jack to "Keep boring in. Keep pounding them home until he folds up." Dempsey wondered if his manager understood how hard this strategy actually was. Sharkey was much tougher and formidable than either of them had perceived before the bout. Not only was Sharkey a very good puncher, he was an excellent boxer as well.

In the seventh round, Dempsey pounded Sharkey's body with hard lefts and rights. Jack may have slipped in a couple of low blows for good measure. Referee Jack O'Sullivan warned Dempsey about landing low punches. Dempsey continued smashing away at Sharkey's midsection. Sharkey turned to the referee to complain about the low blows. Just at that instant, Dempsey let loose a short left hook to Sharkey's jaw. Sharkey's head shot backwards as he crumbled to the canvas. The crowd rose to their feet and shouted hysterically. Sharkey tried desperately to raise himself from the canvas but it was too late. The referee had counted him out. Dempsey rushed over to the fallen victim and lifted him to his feet. Jack noticed an old telegrapher pounding his fists on the ring apron and shouting with delight, "That'll show these bastards that they can't lick us old guys, Jack."

There were vastly different points of view as to whether Dempsey landed low blows during the bout. Grantland Rice, Damon Runyon, Benny Leonard, and W.O. McGeehan claimed that Dempsey definitely landed several low blows. Gene Tunney, Ed Sullivan, James Corbett, and Westbrook Pegler claimed that Jack didn't land any low blows at all.

Jack Sharkey was as surprised as anyone about the outcome of the fight. In fact, after the third round, Sharkey looked out at the crowd below him and yelled, "Here's your cheese champion." Many years later Sharkey recalled with a great deal of embarrassment that "I thought I had him. In the third, fourth, fifth — I knew it was just a matter of time before I knocked him out."

The question as to whether Dempsey had fouled Sharkey remained unresolved. Many believed Dempsey had indeed blatantly landed several low blows while others were under the impression that Sharkey wore his boxing trunks entirely too high above his waist. Dempsey remained convinced that he had won the fight fairly.

The referee, Jack O'Sullivan, claimed that he witnessed only one low blow. Dempsey suggested that he fought a fair fight right up to Sharkey's unexpected demise. "The right hand blows I drove home," the victor claimed, "were fair and square to Sharkey's body. The left hook to the jaw was the finisher." Underscoring the obvious, Jack exclaimed that "There can be no question about the finisher of that punch." When a reporter asked Dempsey why he punched Sharkey as he turned his head to complain to the referee, Jack snapped, "What was I going to do — write him a letter?"

Jim Dawson continued to blast Dempsey about his ineffectiveness in most of the fight with a somewhat inaccurate view of Dempsey's performance. "He was revealed as a shell of himself," Dawson wrote in the *Times*, "a man whose fighting spirit and effectiveness has left him. He has nothing now but the will to fight, minus even the desire. Of him, it can truly be said that his spirit is willing, but the flesh is weak."

Dempsey's popularity soared after his fight with

Sharkey. He enjoyed his return to the spotlight. Not all was well, however, with Estelle. She was deeply upset about Jack's comeback. Jack felt uncomfortable in her presence. He suggested that perhaps she should return to California ahead of him. Jack wanted to make special appearances in several large cities. He feared Estelle's presence might have a dampening effect on his public relations tour.

Tex Rickard was thrilled about the result of the fight. Not only was it perhaps the biggest non-title fight in history, but Dempsey was able to end the fight with one of the most lethal weapons in heavyweight history, an extremely short and powerful left hook. As in his battle with Firpo, Dempsey proved once again that he was fully capable of pulling out a thrilling victory in the face of almost certain defeat. He may have been far past his peak, but his will to win was still solidly intact.

After the Dempsey-Sharkey fight, Jack believed he had a fifty-fifty chance of beating Tunney in a return bout. He thought his legs were much stronger and his wind was better than they had been in his last encounter with the champion. Dempsey was extremely grateful that many fight fans were routing for him to regain the title.

There were rumors floating around that Tunney was seriously considering retiring from the ring. Only a few people were privy to such a notion. Tex Rickard and New York State Athletic Commissioner William Muldoon were aware of Gene's plans to pack it in. Reportedly, Tunney asked Rickard to quickly arrange for a rubber match with Dempsey.

Rickard immediately sprang into action. He got down to business and began negotiating for the site of the next

Dempsey-Tunney fight. Several sports commissioners from states like Massachusetts and New York approached Rickard about staging the fight in their state. James Farley, The New York state commissioner, proposed a top ticket price of $27.50. Rickard refused to deal with Farley because Chicago offered a much higher top ticket price. Furthermore, Rickard was concerned that no arena in New York was large enough to hold the number of spectators he expected to appear for the grand event.

Rickard finally announced that the big fight would be held at Soldier Field in Chicago. The American Legion immediately protested Rickard's choice of venue. They argued that it would be disgraceful to hold a prizefight in a stadium dedicated to the memory of all those American soldiers who had fought and died in the World War.

When Jack arrived home he was shocked to discover that Estelle's condition had grown much worse. Her doctors determined that she might be on the verge of a nervous breakdown. Jack was afraid to begin training for his return bout with Tunney. He refused to leave her while she tried to recover.

Rickard informed Dempsey that advance ticket orders for a second Tunney-Dempsey fight began flooding his office just days after the Dempsey-Sharkey fight. He had never seen anything like it. Dempsey was excited about facing Tunney again, but at the same time he was deeply concerned about his wife's condition.

Estelle slowly recovered. As soon as she was strong enough, Jack and Estelle traveled to Chicago. Dempsey made arrangements for his wife and her nurse to stay at a hotel on the North Side of Chicago. Dempsey stayed with her as often as he could. He was concerned, however, that she might have a relapse once he started training to recapture the title.

Dempsey had difficulty training every day. Some days he trained hard and on other days he lacked the enthusiasm required to get into proper shape for a big heavyweight fight. Dempsey and his manager received word that Tunney was training hard every day, almost as if his life depended on it.

Tunney spoke to a gathering in Chicago about what he thought of the upcoming bout. "The talk seems to be about some fight that is to be held, about which I know nothing. I am here to train for a boxing contest, not a fight. I don't like fighting. Never did. But I'm free to admit that I like boxing." Tunney revealed in his comments his philosophy regarding pugilism. He firmly believed that pummeling an opponent was not the proper way to defeat him. He viewed boxing as a kind of art form in which well thought out ring tactics and strategy should be utilized, not brainlessly slugging away at one's opponent. To many, this sounded like a dig against Jack.

Dempsey grew increasingly concerned about a cut he had received in his battle with Jack Sharkey. The cut was over one eye and it kept opening during his sparring sessions. Jack was worried that the wound wouldn't heal in time for the upcoming bout. He asked Tex Rickard to postpone the fight for about a week. Rickard agreed wholeheartedly. The fight was set to take place on September 22, 1927.

Dempsey's sparring sessions were watched by thousands of excited fans. Jack pounded away at his sparring partners, hurting several of them in the process. Big Boy

Peterson, Allentown Joe Gans, and Whitey Allen all paid a stiff price for getting in the ring with Dempsey. Jack was taking this fight very seriously and acted accordingly. He was not as jovial and fun loving as he had been in earlier training sessions. Dempsey became disheartened when he discovered that Tunney had been guaranteed one million dollars for his upcoming bout. The guarantee was the largest amount in the history of boxing. Dempsey was only guaranteed $450,000 for his participation.

"Scarface" Al Capone spread the word that he was certain Jack would beat Tunney. He claimed that he had enough clout to make it happen. As soon as Dempsey heard about Capone's boast, he sent the mobster a letter requesting Capone not to interfere with the fight in any way. Capone did not reply to Dempsey's request. Shortly after Jack sent his letter to Capone, Estelle received an expensive bouquet of flowers with a card which read, "To the Dempseys, in the name of sportsmanship."

Another unusual event occurred just before the bout. The original referee for the Tunney-Dempsey fight, Dave Miller, was pulled and replaced with Dave Barry. Apparently, Miller had been approached in a restaurant by several men who warned him about who "the boss" was. Shaken by the threat, Miller decided he wanted no part of the fight.

The day of the fight had finally arrived. Dempsey entered the ring first. The crowd cheered loudly as they rose to their feet. The challenger wore black trunks and an old white robe that draped over his broad shoulders. James P. Dawson wrote that "Men and women arose as if pulled erect by some giant magnet." The crowd continued to cheer as Jack danced around the ring and waved to the crowd. Paul Gallico was at ringside and he noted the crowd's adulation toward their hero, Jack Dempsey. Gallico claimed that Tunney's image was that of a "priggish, snobbish, bookish fellow, too proud to associate with common prizefighters."

Tunney received polite applause as he stepped into the ring. The ovation was noticeably less than the one he received a year earlier. It may have been partly due to the fact that Dempsey was now the underdog trying to reclaim the most coveted prize in sports. Many fans quite possibly related to Dempsey as a man trying to regain a semblance of his former self.

Jack greeted Tunney as the champion entered the ring. "How are you, Gene?" the challenger asked Tunney. "Quite well, Jack," Tunney responded with a warm smile. They shook hands and Tunney nodded his head and smiled slightly. The champion wore white trunks and his Marine robe.

A number of former champions were introduced to a crowd of cheering and appreciative fans. Included in the mix were none other than the great Jack Johnson, "Gentleman" Jim Corbett, Battling Nelson, and James J. Jeffries.

The two fighters were called to the center of the ring by referee Dave Barry. He explained to the fighters the essential rules for the fight. One rule in particular would play a significant role in the fight. "Now I want to get one point clear," Barry explained. "In the event of a knockdown, the man scoring the knockdown will go to the farthest neutral corner. Is that clear?" Both fighters acknowledged that they understood the ruling. Emphasizing the importance of the neutral corner ruling, Barry pronounced that "In the event of a knockdown, unless the boy scoring it goes to the far-thest neutral corner, I will not begin the count. When I tell you to break, I want you to break clean. Now shake hands and come out fighting."

The opening bell sounded. Dempsey immediately charged toward Tunney. Jack needed to end the fight quickly because he fully understood he could not out-point Tunney. He needed to destroy Tunney by knocking him out early. Unfortunately for the challenger, Tunney clev-erly fell into a clinch every time Jack tried to land punches. Dempsey charged and Tunney clinched. This sequence of activity between the fighters followed the same pattern as their first fight.

Dempsey later admitted that he should never have entered the ring that night against the seemingly invincible Gene Tunney. By the end of the fourth round, Jack regret-ted his decision to try and regain the title. He was bleeding badly and he appeared thoroughly exhausted. In compari-son, Tunney looked fresh and supremely confident.

In the fifth and sixth rounds, Dempsey rushed Tunney in a desperate attempt to land some blows. Tunney beat Jack to the punch, landing terrific combinations of blows to Dempsey's face. By the end of the sixth round, Dempsey sported a cut near his right eye and his left eye was badly swollen.

In the seventh round, Jack once again charged the champion. Suddenly, Dempsey reached forward and drove Tunney into the ropes with a lunging left hand blow to the champ's jaw. Dempsey quickly followed up his attack with a flurry of punches, ending with a hard right to Gene's jaw. Tunney dropped to the canvas, looking utterly stunned and confused. He shook his head and appeared to say "wow" or a word similar to that as he sat recuperating from the devastating flurry of blows delivered by Dempsey.

Tunney later expressed bitter disappointment regarding the knockdown. "For a boxer of any skill," he wrote, "to be hit with a left swing in a commonplace maneuver of sparring is sheer disgrace." He offered the excuse that perhaps during one of his sparring sessions, he received an eye injury which may have caused a blind spot.

While Tunney recuperated from the knockdown, Dempsey stood behind him in the corner, waiting to unleash more punishment. He had forgotten to go to a neutral corner. Referee Dave Barry shouted to Dempsey to "Get to a neutral corner!" Dempsey ignored Barry's command. Several crucial seconds passed before Dempsey finally moved to a corner away from the fallen champion. At that point, Barry began the count.

Tunney later remarked that he remembered nothing about the conversation that took place between referee Dave Barry and Dempsey. Perhaps he may have been semi-unconscious at that moment or he was totally focused on surviving Dempsey's next assault.

The champion had never been knocked down in the ring prior to this bout. But because he was such an intelligent boxer, he may have determined well before the fight what plan of action would probably work best if he were ever knocked down by Dempsey. One option would be to fall into a clinch as soon as he got to his feet. Tunney may have reasoned, however, that Jack was extremely lethal at very close range. He could hurt you with short blows to the body and head. Tunney decided to avoid Dempsey altogether by back-pedaling as quickly as possible. He knew Dempsey was too slow to catch up with him.

Tunney jumped up at the count of nine and immediately backpedaled away from the charging Dempsey. "Come on and fight!" Jack shouted at Tunney. As the round progressed, Dempsey grew tired of chasing Tunney around the ring. Sensing Jack's weariness, Tunney hit Dempsey with some long-range bombs that stunned the challenger. Dempsey was unable to back Tunney into a corner so he could unleash a deadly barrage of blows. He blindly followed Tunney around the ring trying desperately to unload a knockout blow to Tunney's jaw.

Nat Fleischer, a highly influential authority on boxing, documented his observations regarding what he had witnessed after the knockdown. "Referee Barry raised his hand and was on the verge of starting the count when he noticed that Dempsey was in his own corner which happened to be almost on top of Tunney. It was then that Barry rushed over to Dempsey, grasped him by the arm and urged him to go to a neutral corner. This order Dempsey failed to obey and the penalty followed. It was a command that could be plainly heard at ringside and was heard by me, for I was sitting in the third row of the press box just in front of where Tunney went down. Referee Barry said to Dempsey, 'Go to a neutral corner, Jack.' 'I stay here,' snapped Dempsey, scowling. Tunney was on the floor exactly thirteen seconds, which, with the one second final count as he arose, made the full count fourteen seconds. This was the official announcement of Paul Beeler, the official knockdown timekeeper. I have always felt that Gene Tunney was not in a helpless condition and that he could have arisen any time after the first four seconds and then it is problematical whether Dempsey could have put him away."

Tunney remembered the knockdown very vividly and wrote about it in a book. "In the seventh round, after some fifty seconds of jabbing, feinting and missing, I led a straight left which Dempsey crossed with a long right. This hit me high. I realized it, so did Dempsey. I danced back a step or two. Dempsey followed. With a long, left swinging hook, he hit me on the right side of the chin. It was a savage punch and shook me up. Suddenly a right followed which I partially rode. My back was to the ropes. I leaned against them quite relaxed. Rebounding with a spring I raised my guard. Dempsey slipped in with another left hook that got inside my guard and hit me as I sprang from the ropes. This blow had the added force of catching me as I hurled myself forward. It landed again on the right side of the chin. It was a terrific blow. I began sagging against the ropes. It was the fourth he had landed in quick succession. As I slowly crumbled to the canvas, being partially supported and held up by the ropes, he followed with a hard right, a left, and another right. By the time the last right landed, I was just short of sitting on the canvas. Seven vicious punches in all. I have no recollection of the last three. This was the first time in my life I had ever been knocked down."

Immediately after Tunney rose to his feet, Dempsey charged at Tunney, determined to put him away for good. Tunney simply back-pedaled and side-stepped away from Jack. Unfortunately for Dempsey, he apparently was not proficient in the strategy of cutting off the ring and thereby cornering one's opponent.

Jimmy Bronson, Tunney's corner man, screamed

at Gene not to be so careless with Dempsey. "I told him plenty before the eighth round started," Bronson acknowledged. "I had just warned him to keep away from that one-two punch when he walked right into it. When he came back, I called him everything I could think of and all he said was, 'I'm all right, Jimmy, don't worry.' And he was. He showed that by fighting the smart battle that he did."

Tunney later reminisced about perhaps the most famous seventh round in the history of boxing. "I started a left lead," Gene recalled, "and Dempsey crossed his right over it. I didn't see the left coming. So far as I was concerned it came from out of nowhere. That embarrassed me more," Tunney confessed, "than anything else, not to mention the damage done."

By the eighth round, Tunney was in complete control of the fight. Blows rained upon Dempsey's head as he tried to protect himself. Toward the end of the eighth round, Dempsey grew careless and opened himself up as an easy target. Tunney hit Dempsey with a left hook to the jaw and the challenger dropped to one knee. Curiously, the referee immediately began counting over Jack even though Tunney had not retreated to a neutral corner as he should have. It was one of those moments that didn't stir up any controversy but should have. Jack quickly rose to his feet. Tunney continued pounding Dempsey with highly effective, long-range bombs. In the ninth and tenth round, Dempsey received more punishment from Tunney. He was unable to launch any kind of effective offence. It appeared Jack was just trying to survive the rest of the fight.

Tunney was declared the winner over Dempsey. He had officially won seven of the ten rounds. Jack felt thoroughly disgusted by his performance. He couldn't wait to get out of the ring and out of Chicago. Tunney received $990,445.54 for his efforts against Jack. In order to receive a check for one million dollars, the champion wrote out a personal check for $9,554.46 to Tex Rickard. Rickard was now able to provide Tunney with a million-dollar check, unheard of for its time.

Jack "Doc" Kearns, Jack's relentless nemesis, was upset that Dempsey had lost the fight. "The judges and referee," he claimed, "had nothing to do with the result. His handlers should have shooed him away. Were I on the job, I would have had Jack out of the ring on his way to the dressing room, instead of waiting for Referee Barry to shoo Jack to his corner. At any rate, Referee Barry definitely should have given Jack the benefit of the four second already counted instead of starting the count over again."

Dave Barry related his views regarding Tunney's condition immediately after the knockdown in the infamous seventh round. "My impression of Tunney after he had been knocked down," Barry recalled, "was that he had regained his senses in three or four seconds, and even had Dempsey immediately retired to a neutral corner, Tunney would have been able to rise in good shape before the final count. I think it was a great fight and there is no doubt about who won it."

Kearns continued to gloat about how Dempsey would have been declared the winner had he been in Jack's corner that night in Chicago. "Had I been in Dempsey's corner that night, I'd have landed into the ring as I did in Toledo and I'd have taken Jack out and this time I would not have gotten him to return to resume the fight."

The controversy surrounding the "long count" that occurred in the seventh round never subsided. Tex Rickard and all the major sportswriters were thrilled to have something to argue about in their syndicated columns. Many boxing fans were convinced that Dempsey might have been cheated out of a victory over Tunney. The only remedy in many people's minds was a rematch. Naturally, Rickard sided with the disenchanted fight fans.

Jack wrote about the infamous round seven in a book called simply, *Dempsey*. "Round seven was the round that made the fight, the round I shall never forget simply because it created more than fifty years of controversy. A powerful right followed by a left hook and then by more blows sent Tunney to the canvas with a look of bewilderment on his face. I forgot the rules. I lost my head and couldn't move as Referee Barry shouted, 'Get to a neutral corner!' I stayed put. The count had already started when I was pushed toward a neutral corner, already having lost valuable seconds. I was the jungle fighter so completely set in my ways I couldn't accept new conditions. I was used to standing over my opponents to make sure that when I pounded them down, they stayed down. The count stopped and started again at one. At nine, Tunney was up. He then pedaled around the ring keeping out of my exhausted reach."

Dempsey also defended Gene regarding his reaction to being knocked down. "There have been millions of words written about how he went on the bicycle after that. That's a lot of hooey. Sure, be backed up until he got his bearings. Then he continued to beat me. He had been winning on points up to then almost as in the first fight. I chased him and couldn't keep up. Tired, I set my feet and beckoned to him to come in and fight. That seems pretty silly when I look back on it, though a lot of guys wrote some nice things about that. Why should he do what I wanted him to do?"

Reportedly, Al Capone told two of Tunney's friends, "I lost forty-five grand on the fight, but I don't give a damn because Tunney is from New York. Before the fight, I heard Tunney was up in his training camp with a lot of lavender boys in golf clothes and that they didn't know what it was all about. So I says this to the guys who told me to bet as much as I wanted on Dempsey and that everything was okay." Apparently, Capone was under the false impression that "college boys" were in charge of training Gene for the fight and that Tunney was spending too much time reading books and not enough time on sparring and roadwork.

A crowd of 104,943 spectators attended the second Dempsey-Tunney fight. The receipts for the championship title fight totaled a mind-boggling $2,858,660, making it the fifth million-dollar gate. No sane individual could possibly predict a sporting event as monumental as this one in the foreseeable future.

CHAPTER NINE

THE LEGEND BEGINS

Jack Dempsey in retirement as he stands alongside the great ex-heavyweight champion Jack Johnson.

After the second Dempsey-Tunney fight, Jack's popularity soared to new heights. Paul Gallico observed that Jack was now regarded as the "greatest and most beloved sports hero the country had ever known." People understood that Dempsey was way past his prime, but he never stopped trying to defeat a younger and much more astute boxer. Perhaps fans understood what it's like to try one's best, only to come up short in the end. Gallico believed that Jack Dempsey's defeat "made him human and one of us." Dempsey never publicly complained about his failure to regain the title. He shrugged and proclaimed that "It was just one of the breaks. Tunney fought a smart fight."

Tex Rickard desperately wanted a third Tunney-Dempsey fight. He was certain the next super event would be even bigger than the first two. Many Dempsey fans thought that their hero should have won by a knockout over Tunney in the seventh round and that he was essentially robbed of the heavyweight title. Rickard assured Jack he would receive a million-dollar guarantee for his next encounter with Tunney.

Dempsey told Nat Fleischer that Tunney had offered him a third shot. Dempsey declined Tunney's offer because he was deeply concerned about his vision. His eye specialist had warned Jack that his "eyesight will be impaired to a dangerous point" if he continued to fight. Jack agreed with his doctor's suggestion not to return to the ring. It can be argued that even if Dempsey had won the second fight, he may very well have lost to Gene in a third bout because Tunney was a superior boxer and he probably would have learned from his mistakes.

"Had I desired to continue boxing," Dempsey told Fleischer, "Rickard would have been the promoter. He told me so. He said a third bout would have drawn the biggest crowd in ring history. However, I wasn't interested in fighting Gene again."

Dempsey was not interested in suffering yet another one-sided, embarrassing loss to Tunney. He didn't want to end his career with a record of losing three times to the same fighter. Even if he was able to successfully get himself into shape, he didn't want to risk losing his eyesight. His doctor warned him that any further damage to his eye could lead to blindness.

The heavyweight division, the most prestigious division in all of boxing, was in terrible shape after Dempsey's retirement. Tex Rickard was well aware of the fact that the only top heavyweight contenders were not good for the gate. Names like Tom Heeney of New Zealand, Jack Delaney, and Johnny Risko, who hailed from Cleveland, didn't exactly set the world on fire. Rickard did his best, however, to promote Gene Tunney as a great heavyweight champion. In January of 1928, Rickard tried to sell Tunney to the public.

"There is no denying that Tunney is not only a champion," he claimed, "but a great champion. I believe that he is one of the greatest champions the class has seen. Any man who saw Dempsey make the most desperate effort of his entire career and send Tunney down, and then saw Tunney come out of this crisis and fight back until he hurt his man, must admit that in Gene Tunney the American ring has developed another outstanding exponent of science, power, gameness, and sportsmanship."

What Rickard understood but didn't admit publicly

was the fact that there simply was no one in the heavy-weight division who could compare to Dempsey's ruth-lessness in the ring. Gene Tunney was indeed a supreme boxer, but he didn't possess the attributes many fight fans had admired in Jack Dempsey. Tunney did not stalk and destroy his opponents as Dempsey did. Instead, Tunney beat his opponents with clever boxing.

Amazingly, Gene Tunney announced his plans for retirement not long after Dempsey announced his retire-ment. Tunney may have sensed that without Dempsey, his main nemesis, he might have difficulty drawing fans to his fights. Tunney was a brilliant boxer, but he lacked what many boxing fans wanted in their champion, namely a vicious, no holds barred stalker.

On July 26, 1928, Tunney faced New Zealander Tom Heeney in New York City. Tex Rickard had hoped that the gate receipts would be in the ball park of one million dollars. He was in for a sorry disappointment. The fight still drew about forty-five thousand fans. Dempsey was introduced to the crowd before the fight. As he bowed to the fans, they responded with an unbelievable ovation of cheers.

Heeney managed to land some very hard punches at the champion, but Gene was never in any real danger. The champion finally knocked out the New Zealander in the seventh round. The fight grossed $674,950, but Rickard lost $150,000 of his own money. Tunney did well for himself, however, raking in a cool $525,000 and Heeney walked away with $100,000.

Rickard convinced Dempsey that they should become business partners. Jack immediately agreed to the idea. The two partners traveled to Miami to promote the

Sharkey-Stribling fight. Rickard asked Jack if he would consider fighting the winner of the match. Dempsey remained noncommittal to the suggestion and nothing more was said.

One morning in January of 1929, Rickard woke up complaining of a terrible pain in his stomach. He also felt extremely nauseous. A doctor prescribed antacids for what he believed was indigestion. Later that day Rickard developed a very high fever. He was immediately rushed to the nearest hospital. His fever was so high that his bedsheets were soaked with his sweat. Jack received word that one of the Mayo brothers was in Havana. Jack contacted the doctor and asked him to diagnose his friend. Mayo assured Jack that Rickard was in very good hands.

On January 6, 1929, Tex Rickard, perhaps the greatest boxing promoter of all time, passed away as Jack held his best friend's hand for the last time. Dempsey was utterly devastated. He wept uncontrollably as he tried to hide his face. Tex Rickard's body laid in state in Madison Square Garden. Thousands of fans paid their last respects to their fallen hero as they walked past his casket. Jack was the last bereaver to leave the Garden out of respect to his dearest and closest friend.

The man in charge of the Madison Square Garden, William F. Carey, strongly suggested to Dempsey that he should continue his promotion of the Sharkey-Stribling fight in Florida. Jack wholeheartedly agreed, partly because it was a joint venture between Rickard and himself and he wanted to see it through to the end in memory of Tex. Al Capone showed up for the fight. He bet big money on Sharkey to win and he wanted to be there in person to collect his winnings. Sharkey won a 10 round decision.

Back in California, Estelle was as mad as ever over her husband's notoriety. She thought that as long as she remained with Dempsey, their lives would be under close scrutiny by gossip columnists and sportswriters from all over the country. The couple began spending more time away from each other. Estelle despised Jack's friends and badgered him about it.

Dempsey was very well off financially in 1929, and he wasn't the only one. On the surface, the American economy was booming. The Dow Jones Industrial Index continued to rise higher each week. Jack's financial advisors advised him to purchase more real estate and shares of stocks. They suggested that he buy on margin, or borrowed money, in order to own as many shares as possible. Jack listened to their advice and eagerly bought more assets.

Dempsey also went into partnership with several businessmen who wanted to develop a million-dollar Mexican resort in Baja, California. The resort would include a casino, clubhouses, and a one-mile pier. Jack was instrumental in obtaining a twenty-year concession from the Mexican government.

In October of 1929, the stock market unexpectedly went into a tailspin. There appeared to be no bottom to the stock market as anxious speculators desperately sold shares of everything they owned. Dempsey and many investors watched in horror as their overvalued investments tanked. Jack tried to unload all of his shares of equites in order to cut his losses short. In the end, Dempsey calculated that he had lost over three million dollars.

One morning, Estelle turned to Jack as they laid in

bed together and said, "I've had it. Get out of my life and stay out. I want a divorce." Jack tried to console her but she refused to back down from her demand. Jack promptly moved out of the house and into a hotel. To help keep his mind off his failed marriage, Dempsey managed the Playa Ensenada Hotel in Baji. At first, the resort attracted high rollers from America and Europe. Late in December, however, Jack realized that the resort was on the brink of financial ruin. In just a very short period of time, expenses totaled an astounding two million dollars, with no end in sight. The investment was rapidly hemorrhaging money. Angry vendors demanded immediate payment for their services.

Like many Americans, Dempsey desperately needed money. Unlike most of the folks who suffered from the effects of the depression, Dempsey was able to take advantage of his star power. He even seriously considered meeting Max Schmeling in the ring. Jack's new fight manager, Leonard Sacks, set up a series of exhibition bouts for Jack. In just thirty days, Dempsey fought forty-two challengers in thirteen cities. He earned a cool quarter of a million dollars. Dempsey proved to be a bankable commodity. The exhibition tour was difficult for Jack. He was quite a bit older than many of his rivals. He frequently faced as many as five opponents in one night of boxing. Jack refereed boxing matches which allowed him to make considerably more money.

In September of 1931, Jack and Estelle were officially divorced. The divorce settlement allowed Estelle to receive $40,000 in cash, a furnished home worth $150,000, and three automobiles. Even right after the divorce, Jack was willing to get back with Estelle. She was too envious and resentful of Jack to even consider returning to him. Dempsey decided to simply forget her and move on with his life.

According to Dempsey, he faced 175 fighters in the ring between August 20, 1931 and August 15, 1932. It wasn't unusual for him to battle four fighters in one night. Jack calculated that he knocked out over a hundred fighters during that period. Dempsey began to believe that maybe he could make a comeback. Sportswriters insisted that he could still punch hard.

Dempsey continued to fight exhibition bouts and referee in order to pay the bills. He discovered that he was still able to draw massive crowds to his events. Convinced that he might have a chance to return to the ring, he agreed to fight Kingfish Levinsky, a respectable heavyweight boxer. One big drawback for Dempsey, however, was the fact that he was now thirty-seven and his challenger was only twenty-one.

The two fighters met on February 18, 1932, in the Chicago Stadium for a four-round exhibition. Levinsky out-boxed Dempsey in every round. The younger man tied Jack up so often that Dempsey was unable to land any effective punches. Dempsey concluded right after the fight that he was just a shell of his former self. The sportswriters who witnessed the "fight" agreed with Dempsey that his fighting days were over.

Dempsey was thankful for finding out that his professional fighting days were definitely over. Had he pressed the issue he probably would have been allowed to fight Jack Sharkey for the title. After his miserable performance in the Levinsky bout, he knew Sharkey was fully capable of knocking him out.

In 1933 Prohibition was no longer the law of the

land. The well-intentioned experiment became just a bad memory to most Americans. Franklin Delano Roosevelt became President of the United States after soundly defeating Herbert Hoover the year before. Unemployment hovered around 25 percent as many hard-working Americans were reduced to selling apples on street corners.

Dempsey was still good box office. He was frequently featured in several popular and not so popular movies, including, *The Prizefighter and the Lady*, and *Mr. Broadway*. The former film also featured heavyweight boxers Jess Willard, Max Baer, and Primo Carnera. Jack was actually brought into the production to keep Max Baer and Primo Carnera from fighting each during the filming of the picture.

Jack started dating Hannah Williams. She was famous for singing a song called "Cheerful Little Earful." Jack fell in love with Hannah and told her he wanted to marry her. He told Hannah that she would need to forsake her career in the entertainment business if she wanted to marry him. Evidently, he didn't want to relive another bad marriage with a starlet. Hannah filed for divorce from bandleader-aviator Roger Kahn. Dempsey laid low so as not to cause trouble during the divorce proceedings which took place in Reno, Nevada. In 1933 Jack and Hannah were married in Elko, Nevada by Justice of the Peace A.J. MacFarland. Hannah promised to give up show business in order to raise a family and take care of her new husband.

Dempsey opened a restaurant near Madison Square Garden in 1935. It was an immediate success. Jack Dempsey's restaurant was later moved to a new location on the west side of Broadway. The ex-champion frequently sat by the restaurant's front window and he made it a point of greeting awe inspired customers as they entered his establishment. The restaurant went out of business in 1974.

After a rocky relationship, Jack was granted a divorce from Hannah in 1943. He was also awarded custody of his two daughters. Jack felt bad for Hannah and promised that he would do all he could to support her. She was, after all, the mother of his only children and she deserved a helping hand. Jack was hit with more tragedy when his mother died. According to her doctor, Celia remained feisty to the bitter end. She threatened to punch him in the face if he didn't stop caring for her so much.

In 1941 Dempsey tried to enlist in the military but was turned down due to his age. Jack didn't give up, however. The Coast Guard gratefully placed him in charge of physical fitness training at Manhattan Beach in Brooklyn. Jack was part of the American assault on Okinawa in 1945. He was forty-nine years old at the time of the successful attack.

On January 30, 1950, Dempsey was guest of honor at the Boxing Manager's Guild Dinner at the Hotel Edison in New York City. Jack had recently been voted the greatest prize fighter of the first half-century by sportswriters and sportscasters. The poll had been conducted by the Associated Press. Jack Kearns was also an honored guest at the dinner. Kearns' presence made Jack uncomfortable. As Dempsey entered the hotel ballroom he was bombarded with requests for his autograph. Over one thousand cheering admirers stood up and greeted Jack.

Dempsey stood behind the podium and spoke these words:

"I will be grateful to Kearns all my life for making me a champion. Kearns told me I was the greatest fighter in

THE MILLION DOLLAR MAN

the world and I believed him. He told me I was a terrific puncher and I believed him. He had me breaking doors with punches."

"On the morning of the Jess Willard fight Kearns came to me and said he had bet $10,000 to $100,000 I'd win by a knockout in the first round. He told me I was going to knock out Willard. I believed him."

"Gentlemen, Jack Kearns made me a million dollars."

After Jack's gracious speech, Dempsey and Kearns shook hands for the first time in many years.

"This means more to me than Maxim winning a dozen titles," Kearns told Jack. "Everybody had always known my heart belonged to Dempsey," Kearns added.

On that very night, Jack forgave Kearns for all his transgressions against him. But he would never forget the anguish Kearns put Jack through after their breakup.

On January 8, 1964, Dempsey was told about a scathing article in a forthcoming issue of *Sports Illustrated*. Jack Kearns had recently written a memoir that was due for release. In the book, Kearns made the unsubstantiated assertion that Dempsey's gloves were "loaded" with plaster just before the Willard-Dempsey fight in 1919.

Dempsey immediately sent a letter to the editors of *Sports Illustrated* and threatened them with a lawsuit. Unfazed by Dempsey's warning, the magazine hit the newsstands on January 13. Many of the fans who were at the fight in Toledo claimed they never saw anything suspicious before, during, or after the fight. Manufacturers of plaster indicated that if Dempsey had indeed used plaster, his hands would have been seriously injured from just one blow.

Jack sued the magazine for libel, sensibly claiming that

his reputation had been viciously tarnished. Jack's attorneys further indicated that "freedom of the press is not a license for profit at the expense of others." An out of court settlement was reached and Jack received a formal apology.

Dempsey's health took a turn for the worse in the 1970s. He experienced a series of strokes. He no longer enjoyed relatively good health for a man his age. He had difficulty remembering his past glories in the ring. He was eventually fitted with a pacemaker because of his weak heart. Sadly, his health continued to deteriorate over the years. On May 31, 1983, William Harrison "Jack" Dempsey passed away at age 87 primarily due to natural causes. He was buried in the Southampton Cemetery in Southampton, New York.

To many, Jack Dempsey's achievement in the ring was proof that any man who possessed grit and determination could make it in America. At a very early age, Jack had a singular, unbridled passion to become a championship prizefighter. He was determined that nothing and no one would stand in his way, at least not for very long. He went on to become America's first iconic sports hero. The sheer ferociousness he exhibited in the ring was unequaled in his era, and many would argue, in any era. He once summed up his fight philosophy with the quote, "A champion is someone who gets up when he can't." The thrills and excitement Jack Dempsey brought to the sport of boxing cannot and will not be forgotten for all time.

BIBLIOGRAPHY

Cavanaugh, Jack. *Tunney*. New York: Random House, 2006

Dempsey, William Harrison. *Round by Round*. New York: Whittlesey House, 1940

Dempsey, Jack as told to Bob Considine and Bill Slocum. *Dempsey*. New York: Simon and Schuster, 1960

Dempsey, Jack with Barbara Piattelli Dempsey. *Dempsey*. New York: Harper & Row, Publishers, 1977

Evensen, Bruce J. *When Dempsey Fought Tunney*. Tennessee: The University of Tennessee Press, 1996

Fleischer, Nat. *Jack Dempsey*. New York: Arlington House, 1972

Jarrett, John. *Gene Tunney: The Golden Guy Who Licked Jack Dempsey Twice*. London: Robson Books, 2003

Jarrett, John. *Dempsey and the Wild Bull*. Durrington: Pitch, 2015

Kahn, Roger. *A Flame of Pure Fire*. New York: Harcourt Brace & Company, 1999

Kearns, Jack (Doc). *The Million Dollar Gate*. New York: The Macmillan Company, 1966

Kelly, Jason. *Shelby's Folly: Jack Dempsey, Doc Kearns, and the Shakedown of a Montana Boomtown*. Nebraska: University of Nebraska Press, 2010

Pietrusza, David. *Rothstein: The Life, Times, and Murder of the Criminal Genius Who Fixed the 1919 World Series.* New York: Basic Books, 2003

Rickard, Mrs. "Tex." *Everything Happened To Him.* New York: Frederick A. Stokes Company, 1936

Roberts, Randy. *Jack Dempsey: The Manassa Mauler.* Chicago: University of Illinois Press, 1979

Samuels, Charles. *The Magnificent Rube: The Life and Times of Tex Rickard.* New York: McGraw-Hill Book Company, Inc., 1957

Schoor, Gene. *The Jack Dempsey Story.* New York: Julian Messner, Inc., 1954

Smith, Toby. *Kid Blackie: Jack Dempsey's Colorado Days.* Colorado: Wayfinder Press, 2003

Waltzer, Jim. *The Battle of the Century: Dempsey, Carpentier, and the Birth of Modern Promotion.* California: Praeger, 2011

INDEX

Printed in the USA
CPSIA information can be obtained
at www.ICGtesting.com
LVHW041308220924
791612LV00002B/37

9 781587 904011